The Badass Girl's Guide

Uncommon Strategies to Outwit Predators

CJ Scarlet

ISBN: 1977667716
ISBN 13: 9781977667717
Library of Congress Control Number: 2017915188
CreateSpace Independent Publishing Platform
North Charleston, South Carolina

Table of Contents

The One Book Predators Don't Want You to Read!

DEAR READER, I am so happy and honored that you're reading this book! Whether you're a survivor of assault, someone who wants to protect themselves and those they care about, or the loved one of someone who wants to protect *you*, I promise you'll be savvier and more empowered by reading these pages.

The Badass Girl's Guide: Uncommon Strategies to Outwit Predators is the one book criminal predators don't want you to read! Filled with critical information about how to empower yourself to keep from becoming a crime statistic, this definitive, comprehensive guide contains facts and strategies not found in other personal security books.

From tips on how to "fail" the predator interview and avoid being targeted, to instructions on using your personal bodily "weapons" to defend yourself in a confrontation, I offer everything you need to know to stay safe, fight if you must (without knowing any martial arts or formal self-defense techniques), and navigate the criminal justice system if the worst happens.

While there's no shame in complying with the demands of a predator if you decide that's your safest bet, I focus more in this book on how to fight back against perpetrators and how that can be done. The information I provide about how to make a report to police or your Title IX administrator, how to get a rape kit exam, and how to navigate the criminal justice system are meant for every reader.

I also have two bonuses for you: (1) I added a short story to the end of this book that I wrote more than two decades ago called *Escape from the Terrible Garden.* This story was written when I was working through my own issues with victimization. Many of you will relate to the woman in the story, who lives in the terrible garden and wants desperately to escape. (2) I'm adding short videos on my website at www.cjscarlet.com that actually show you many of the techniques I suggest in this book. On the website, you can also request my top *7 Secrets You MUST Know to Protect Your Badass Bod from Predators* that you can share with those you care about.

#Me Too

I was 19, a freshman in college, when I was raped by a sheriff's deputy I had just started dating. In 1980 there was no word for date rape, so I blamed myself for "tempting him" by entering his apartment. Then, four months later, I was sexually assaulted by my Marine Corps recruiter, who took advantage of his position of power and authority over me.

For a decade I grappled with the trauma of these events. I had already survived childhood molestations, so these latest assaults manifested an even deeper level of shame and self-loathing. I came to accept I must have a big "V" tattooed on my forehead that announced to every predator within a mile that I was an ideal victim.

Eventually, I found healing through therapy, self-help books, and long talks (and crying jags) into the night with supportive friends, and somewhere along the way I came to love and forgive myself and even my assailants. But the real turning point for me came when I grew tired of the trauma owning my life.

I took my power back and became an advocate for others who had been victimized. I served on the board of the local rape crisis center and took the helm as Executive Director of a child advocacy center, both while working to complete my master's degree in human violence. I then served for three years as Director of Victims Issues for the North Carolina Attorney General's Office, where I implemented the first statewide automated victim notification system that notifies survivors before their perpetrators are released from custody.

Yet, after nearly three decades as a victim advocate, I grew tired of dealing with crime and violence *after* they occurred. I knew that if things continued as they were, the work would never end. I realized that to create genuine change, I needed to address the source of the problem. So, I chose to focus my efforts on thwarting predators and keeping people from being victimized at all.

From the first page to the last, *The Badass Girl's Guide* is important to your safety and possibly your very life, and I hope you'll read every word. Please share this book with everyone you care about. You can never tell when one piece of wisdom found within will be exactly what you or your loved one needs to escape a dangerous situation.

You ARE worth fighting for!

A few disclaimers

You will note that throughout the book I use female pronouns to refer to victims and male pronouns to refer to perpetrators. Sadly, males also are victimized (at a rate close to that of women, according to some studies) and women, too, can perpetrate assaults. This book, while using mainly female pronouns, has much to offer anyone who wants to protect themselves.

The terms "rape" and "sexual assault" are used interchangeably in our society and in this book.

I refer to people who have been victimized as "victims" in some instances and as "survivors" in others, according to where the term is used in the book. I use "survivor" whenever I can to indicate that one has, literally, survived the assault and is on the path to recovery and healing.

To be clear, when I talk about victim dynamics in this book, I am in no way suggesting that being victimized is a failure on the part of the survivor. While some people make better targets because they're vulnerable and/or unprepared or unable to protect themselves, it's NEVER their fault. It's always the criminal's wrong actions that are to blame. Period.

This book arms you with great ways to protect yourself, but every criminal situation is different and you must use your best judgment about if, when, and how to apply the principles you'll learn. Only you can decide how to respond in a given situation to come out of it with the least amount of harm to yourself.

For readers who live outside the United States, the criminal justice systems and processes described here may be different from what you will experience in your community. Ask your prosecutor or victim advocate for information about how the process works in your area.

The names and other details of people featured in this book have been changed to protect their identities.

One final disclaimer—this book was written to protect you. If you faithfully use the techniques contained within these pages, you'll likely minimize dangerous encounters and be safer. However, it cannot hope to end all crime for all time; no book can protect every person in every situation. Use the ideas in this book when you can, and your common sense and best judgment always. I hope you make it a habit to use the recommended psychological techniques I share and that you never have to use the physical moves I suggest.

Thank you so much for reading *The Badass Girl's Guide*. Peace!

CHAPTER 1

"Nice" is a Four-Letter Word

"We talk about how many women were raped last year, not about how many men rape women. We talk about how many girls in a school district were harassed last year, not how many boys harassed girls. We talk about how many teenagers in the state of Vermont got pregnant last year, rather than how many men and boys impregnated teenage girls.

"So, you can see how the use of the passive voice has a political effect. [It] shifts the focus off men and boys and onto girls and women. Even the term 'violence against women' is problematic. It's a passive construction; there's no active agent in the sentence. It's a bad thing that happens to women, but when you look at that term 'violence against women,'

nobody's doing it to them. It just happens to them...
Men aren't even part of it!"

JACKSON KATZ
ACTIVIST ON THE ISSUES OF GENDER, RACE AND VIOLENCE[1]

I DON'T KNOW about you, but I was raised to be nice to everyone. I was taught to avoid being rude at all cost. To smile through awkward situations. To giggle when I felt uncomfortable rather than risk embarrassing someone who was just "playing" with me. To be flattered when a boy hit me on the playground because it meant he "liked" me. To subsume my needs in favor of others' needs. To expect men to be my rescuers if I was in danger. Basically, to be a good girl and not make trouble for anyone.

How many times in your life have you ignored the blaring sirens from your intuition and sat silently as someone violated your boundaries? Or worried as the creepy guy from your dorm followed you to class? Or suffered through regular sexual harassment at work? I sure did; more times than I can count and all in the name of being polite.

Many of us were raised on a steady diet of Cinderella, trashy romance novels, and movies in which the female leads were helpless victims who breathlessly waited for rugged masculine characters to save them. Movies with strong female characters who fought back against their attackers were almost non-existent.

It's a strange paradox—we spend so much of our lives being hypervigilant about potential danger, but become utterly helpless when we're confronted with uncomfortable or dangerous situations. We smile when someone pays us an inappropriate compliment at work. We roll our eyes when a man makes a crude joke or gesture. We stiffen but don't necessarily move when someone brushes up against us.

Why? Why do we "make nice" when we're treated with disrespect? Our instincts are correct, but we override them because our early training was so strong. Part of the reason is fear—that the situation will escalate if we object, that we'll embarrass the other person or ourselves, or that the person we confront won't like/love/employ us anymore. We're also often clueless about how to respond. Then there's the pervasive, personally-held belief that we can't take care of ourselves, so we demure rather than react.

If we did trust our intuition as children and speak up, we may have been told we were overreacting or we were ignored. In some cases, we may even have been punished for saying bad things about Uncle Joe.

All this leads us to feel helpless, which leads to a sense of hopelessness and powerlessness. Denial is also a huge factor; we deny what's happening to us in favor of making excuses for the perpetrator: "He was just kidding." "I'm just being overly sensitive." "He didn't mean it." Or, my (least) favorite, "Boys will be boys." This unfortunate perspective lets men off the hook when they behave badly.

The "Victim" Tattoo

If you read the Introduction, you know my story. I was what is known as a serial victim—someone who was victimized multiple times, in my case because of a history of childhood molestations that left me more vulnerable and made me doubt my own instincts when it came to danger. It also led me to engage in risky behavior that put me smack in the path of predators.

What I know now, after years seeking help for my own personal traumas and advocating for others, is that I was unconsciously sending signals to predators through my body language and behavior that I was a good target.

Even worse, in cases where I knew the perpetrators, I would work to make them feel better about what they'd done because I didn't want them to feel badly about themselves. My attempts to reassure my assailants were my way of maintaining a measure of control over the situation (this behavior is called "fawning," which I address in Chapter 2). After all, if I consciously admitted that someone I trusted was intentionally hurting me, I would have to do something about it, and if I did, one of two things might happen: (1) they would get angry and not like/love me anymore, or (2) they would get violent and hurt me even worse.

Sounds bizarre, right? It's not; it's a well-known phenomenon among serial victims. I believed there was something inherently wrong with me that made good people do bad things, and it seemed obvious bad things would happen to me.

(Note: If you live with the belief that you are inherently flawed in some way and that people would reject you if they could see who you "really are," I urge you to read my bonus story, Escape from the Terrible Garden, which appears at the end of this book. I promise *it will shift your thinking and help you see yourself differently and with greater compassion. You are not alone!)*

The very idea that society in general, and our parents in particular, raise us to be polite regardless of the situation and to blame ourselves first outrages me. After all, why should we spare the perpetrators' feelings when they clearly don't give a damn about ours? They're the ones who ignore and disrespect our boundaries, and it's our right to confront them and protect ourselves!

Well, I've traded in my polite "V" (for victim) tattoo—the apparently invisible imprint on my forehead that predators could clearly see—for a mental "Back off!!" attitude that has kept me safe for nearly three decades now.

We Are Thwarting Our Own Happiness

An alarming number of women and girls, even those who've never been victimized, state that they feel a general sense of self-loathing and shame. And for those who have been victimized, add self-blame to that toxic mix.

As a result, we give away our power to others and allow them to dictate our lives. Yes, we do. Every time we let someone lead us into a decision we're not comfortable with, or allow them to violate our boundaries, we're relinquishing our power.

These feelings are at the heart of why we remain so vulnerable to predators. I'm bringing them to light so you can understand—I mean truly grasp—how this mentality sets us up for victimization. And more than that, this self-defeating mindset serves to deny us the joy of self-love and self-esteem that are essential to living a happy, healthy life.

Ladies, it's time to reject the negative messages bombarding us in the media and society, to be gentle with ourselves, to embrace our perfectly imperfect selves, and claim our power. We must take ownership of and responsibility for our own lives, every single second of them, understanding that we're the only ones who have our best interest in mind at all times.

Taking Our Power Back

When I think back to what enabled me to shed the shame and self-loathing I used to carry, it was when I decided I'd had enough of being taken advantage of and I took my power back! My empowering moment, which didn't happen until I was 35, might appear minor compared to the assaults I'd experienced, but it represented an important shift in my thinking and behavior. I was standing in line at a Dunkin Donuts when I felt the man behind me brush his hand across my backside. First, I stiffened. Then I took a step to the side and barked over my shoulder, "Watch yourself!" That tiny step and warning were the first I'd ever taken to protect myself, and it led to larger steps that helped me become the strong, powerful woman I am today.

If you're tired of feeling afraid, of loathing and blaming yourself, of feeling too vulnerable, then take YOUR power back right now. Yes, right this very second! Recognize that you're a powerful being and claim it!

It's time for you to get indignant! It's time to be as aggressive or rude as necessary to keep yourself safe and secure. It's time to stop waiting for someone else to rescue you. Summon your inner badass and rescue yourself!

And you can do it. By the mere fact that you're human, you possess an innate ability to defend yourself. You were born with this ability, as all animals are, to protect yourself; you just weren't taught to develop those important skills.

Channeling Your Inner Tasmanian Devil

Think you can't protect yourself because you aren't a martial artist? Haven't taken formal self-defense classes? Because you're too old? Physically unfit? Too timid?

Imagine for a moment you decide (and I don't recommend this) to take down that wily squirrel who's been raiding your bird feeder. You sneak up on tiptoe and BOOYAH! You've got the culprit in your hands!

No, what you've got is a whole mess of trouble! Think that squirrel is meekly going to give you control? Hell no! Ms. Squirrel is going to squirm and claw and bite and scratch and fight to get out of your grasp as if her life depended on it. She doesn't care how big you are or how small she is; she's determined to prevail. Even the most skilled black belt would be no match for this one-pound rodent.

That's actually a pretty funny image—Jackie Chan getting his butt kicked by a common brown squirrel—but I want you to take it very seriously because that image might save your life one day.

Better yet, let's use the imagery of the Australian Tasmanian Devil. Although just the size of a small dog, it has the strongest bite of any land mammal and is so ferocious it can repel almost any predator that comes its way. If you recall the old Looney Tunes cartoons, "Taz" is a whirlwind of fists and feet, fangs and raw power. In addition, the real Tasmanian Devil uses a pungent body odor and nerve-racking screech to ward off its enemies.

I explain below how to channel your inner Tasmanian Devil, but first, let's talk about the two types of self-defense you can use to protect yourself.

Psychological and Physical Self-Defense

WHAT IS PSYCHOLOGICAL SELF-DEFENSE?

There are multiple definitions of psychological self-defense, but I'll make it simple: it's everything you think and say to protect yourself, both before, during, and after an assault.

Psychological self-defense is about what happens first, in your mind, and, second, in your behavior and actions to defend yourself. It can range from talking your way out of a bad situation to manipulating the predator to better position yourself to fend him off.

YOU HAVE THE ADVANTAGE!

It's important to appreciate that you have a psychological advantage over your attacker. While you fear him, he's terrified of being caught and you can use his own fear against him. You can shift the power dynamic by making a scene (yelling, for example) to bring attention to the situation—exactly what the predator *doesn't* want.

You can use *your* fear of being victimized as a powerful force to make the criminal afraid! (See more about what predators don't want you to know in Chapter 6).

WHAT IS PHYSICAL SELF-DEFENSE?

Physical self-defense is composed of any actions you take, whether instinctive or learned, to protect yourself in the actual moment of attack. This includes biting, kicking, scratching, gouging, yelling, and anything else you can think of to stop the attacker.

I've taken several self-defense courses over the years and highly recommend them, but with caveats: (1) While I learned many useful moves in each class, there was so much information provided in such a short period that it was overwhelming. Within hours I couldn't remember half the techniques I had learned, and within days, I had forgotten virtually all the correct moves. If you want to get formal training, go for it, but please take several classes so you retain the information. (2) Some of the moves that were taught were, frankly, impractical in real life. In a self-defense course, the "dummy" instructor, usually a man in multiple layers of protective gear, can't go after you the way a real predator would. You'll be taught how to escape a choke hold, for example, but the dummy instructor won't fight you as hard as a real predator would. This could lead to a false sense of your own power. Again, taking multiple classes will help you perfect your movements and lead to greater confidence and better results.

YOUR BODY KNOWS WHAT TO DO

Think it's not in you to fight? Let me ask you this: What would you do if your child or dearest friend were being attacked? Fight like a rabid Tasmanian Devil, I'm betting. You have it in you, I promise, to fight like Taz, and if you do, you increase your chances of getting away from a perpetrator by up to 84 percent.[ii]

Never forget, you always have powerful weapons at your disposal—all contained within the body you walk around in—should you need them in the event of an attack. I'm giving you permission to fight as dirty and unfairly as you can. Go for the predator's weakest spots: the groin, nose, and throat, and anywhere else on his body you can grab or twist to convince him to drop you like a hot rock and run.

Using Your Badass Body to Protect Yourself

Below are just some of the many ways you can use that badass body of yours to protect yourself. (On my website at www.cjscarlet.com, you'll find short videos of these moves to help you better understand how they can be applied.)

Eyes. Looking the potential attacker right in the eyes will help you fail the predator interview (detailed in Chapter 9) by showing him you see him and aren't afraid. This doesn't mean staring him down; rather, you should look at him briefly as you walk by him, perhaps nod in acknowledgement, and move on.

Posture. Your posture tells people a lot about you. Walking confidently with your head up and eyes clear (no texting while walking!) shows predators you're a person to be reckoned with. Studies have been conducted in which convicted criminals were asked to pick out potential targets by looking at videos of them walking down the street. The people who were consistently chosen as potential victims were those who slouched or appeared timid while they walked.

Voice. Your voice is one of the most powerful tools in your self-defense arsenal. You can use it softly to warn the perpetrator to back off, calmly to talk him into leaving you alone, or loudly to freak him out. Many women have talked themselves out of scary situations by being clever ("My boyfriend will be here any minute."), by being friendly ("Cool shoes!"), or by changing the subject ("Do you know where the mall is?"). Yelling fiercely at your attacker or for help will bring attention to your situation. If no one's within hearing distance, your voice will still put the predator off balance and let him know he's not dealing with an easy target.

Head. Whether you're being held from the front or behind, you can swing your head forward or backward into the predator's face or head. Your upper forehead is one of the hardest bones on your body, so don't be afraid to slam it into his nose or chin to snap his head back and give you a chance to get away.

Teeth. My favorite forgotten weapons are your teeth, which inflict excruciating pain to a small area. Bite anything that presents itself to you—skin, ear, face, arm—and the attacker will stop whatever he's currently doing, giving you precious distance and time to get into a better fighting position or flee, if you can.

Elbow. The outside of your lower arm close to the elbow is incredibly strong and effective as a weapon. You can use that area to rapidly strike the predator's face and chest, even his groin and knees if you're below him. Because the elbow is so strong, it will inflict damage to the predator without hurting you much.

Palm. Use the butt of your open palm to hit upward onto predator's chin or nose, which will snap his head back and make his eyes water so you can run away. As with the elbow, your palm can deliver a serious blow without hurting you much, if at all. Even just pushing his chin or nose up with the butt of your hand will force his head back away from you, and possibly enable you to maneuver to a better fighting position.

You can also cup you hand and slap the predator's head or face as hard as you can manage.

Fist. Unless you've trained to do so, punching someone with your fist can be awkward and ineffective. You'd do better using your closed fist and forearm to pound on the attacker like a hammer. (Remember: Keep your thumbs on the outside of your fists or you could break your fingers!)

Fingers. Speaking of fingers, pinching and twisting the predator's skin is *incredibly* painful, especially if you do it on the thin skin of his upper thigh or arms. You can also gouge and scratch the attacker's eyes and skin. Many a predator has been caught because of DNA evidence found under victims' fingernails.

Knees. Use your knee to kick the perpetrator in the groin when you're in close range or smash it into his nose when he's bent over. Keep kneeing him until he falls to the ground so you can run away.

Feet. Your feet can be dangerous when you swipe, stomp, and kick any of his body parts as violently as you can manage.

Again, I go back to the image of Taz who, in the cartoons, is literally a tornado of fury and might. Your battle with a predator doesn't have to win points for form or style; just go completely bonkers and you'll take him by surprise and rattle him, hopefully making him flee the scene in fear for his own life!

Coming Up Next...

In the next chapter, I'll talk about the stages people may go through when they're being attacked, as well as the five ways people respond to fear and how to overcome them in order to move into action. It's important to recognize these stages so you can work through them and choose how to respond to the situation you're confronted with.

CHAPTER 2

How We Respond— or Don't—to Fear

The grainy surveillance video is chilling, even more so because there's no sound. First you see a man leave his car and approach a young woman. He grabs her by the arm and begins to pull her toward his vehicle. She tries to resist by pulling against him, but he's bigger and stronger and she's unable to pull her wrist from his grasp.

At one point, she trips and falls to the ground, but as he continues to pull her wrist, she struggles to her feet and continues to be dragged to his car. It didn't occur to Sheila to simply stay on the ground and fight for her life. It wasn't her fault; she just didn't know the psychological and physical self-defense tools to protect herself.

Three days later, Sheila was found alive, still under the control of the perpetrator. She had been terrorized and repeatedly raped, but she lived through it. The perpetrator was caught and prosecuted, and is serving 35 years in prison.

—∞—

Freeze, Fawn, Flee, Comply, or Fight?

It amuses me when I see television or movie characters acting cool and unfazed when they run into hordes of brain-eating zombies or find their planet under attack by hostile aliens. If such a thing actually happened, we would probably all lose our minds and our hearts would stop in our chests.

Of course, there are people, especially those who've been trained to run toward danger, who would, thank goodness, save the rest of us from inter-planetary destruction. But we can't afford to think we'll miraculously be rescued in *any* situation and we must be prepared to fend for ourselves.

When we first encounter danger, we have one of five reactions: we freeze up, we fawn, we flee, we comply, or we fight. Sometimes we do all five, though not at the same time, of course. In the process, according to authors Chuck O'Neill and Kate O'Neill in their excellent book *Psychological Self-Defense: How to Protect Yourself from Predators, Criminals and Sociopaths Before They Attack*,[iii] we go through four psychological phases when we're attacked. Your job is to move through them as quickly as possible to get to the final phase—anger—where your survival instincts kick into high gear.

The four phases are:

- **Disorientation.** Whether it comes from out of the blue or has escalated slowly to an assault, you're usually disoriented by the attack. The question in your mind in this phase is: "What's happening to me?"
- **Denial and Disbelief.** Your mind will often have trouble believing you're under attack: "I can't believe this is happening!"
- **Depression and Fear.** At this stage, you accept that you're being attacked and you may have depressing and fearful thoughts: "Why is this happening to ME?" or "Am I going to die?"
- **Anger.** This is the stage you want to get to as quickly as possible because it's the one that will likely save you from greatest harm: "Damned if I'm going to let this happen to me!"

Now, let's go through the five actions you might take if you're attacked.

FREEZING

Nearly everybody, unless they've been trained not to, freezes mentally and physically when they're first confronted with a potentially dangerous situation. It's an innate response to danger, but if you stay there you're virtually guaranteed to be victimized.

In the past, I was a freezer, no doubt about it. When confronted with what I considered a frightening situation, I went blank and numb. The blood didn't go to my limbs so I could run or fight, and it most definitely didn't flood my brain so I could think more clearly. Nope, the blood literally left my brain and legs, leaving me wobbly, and unable to see or even hear clearly.

According to research published in the journal *Acta Obstetricia et Gynecologica Scandinavica,*[iv] "tonic immobility"— a state of involuntary but temporary paralysis — is a common reaction for sexual assault victims, making it impossible for them to fight back. Of 298 women surveyed who visited the Emergency Clinic for Rape Victims in Stockholm within one month after being sexually assaulted, 70 percent experienced significant tonic immobility and 48 percent experienced extreme tonic immobility during the assault.

Overcoming the Chemical Cocktail of Fear

Even low levels of the chemicals released when you're confronted with danger—adrenaline and cortisol—can impair your thinking and response time. In this mode, you may not be able to move, think, or even breathe correctly.

Here's what happens to your body when you're attacked:

- When your heart rate goes up to 115 beats per minute as the result of fear (not exercise), your fine motor skills (movements involving small muscles) are impaired, meaning it becomes more difficult to dial your phone for help or unlock your door to escape a predator.
- At 145 beats per minute, your gross motor skills (those involving larger muscle groups) are affected and it becomes difficult to use any self-defense techniques you may have

learned beforehand. *(That's why my advice to summon your inner "Taz" may be your best bet—you don't have to remember any specific formal self-defense or martial arts moves; you just go bonkers, biting and kicking every part of the predator's body you can get to.)*

- At 175 beats per minute, you develop tunnel vision (where your perception is narrowed to a pinpoint), loss of hearing, time distortion (where time slows down or speeds up), and temporary loss of memory (making it hard to recall details of the event for some time afterward).

Yikes!

But wait! There's also good news. Many people who've been attacked say that after the initial freeze period, their minds cleared and their thinking became sharper, enabling them to either see ways to flee the scene or generate the will to fight the attacker until they could escape. The freeze stage can last from seconds to minutes. The faster you can move into fight or flight, the more likely you are to escape.

In my research, I found many books that tell you not to panic and to maintain control in an attack situation. Great advice, but hard to follow in the moment. Panic is almost inevitable initially. When the fear and panic come, acknowledge them and then move as quickly as possible into brainstorming a way out of the situation. Almost anything you can do to escape is better than doing nothing. The important thing is to never give up. As bleak as things may appear, you never know when an opportunity to stop the attack or to escape may present itself.

Here's one of my secrets: I learned a key phrase to help me transition from freezing to fleeing or fighting. The phrase is "5-4-3-2-1 GO!" I practice this in my everyday interactions when I'm confronted by anything that causes me to pause in my thinking. *(I also use it when I don't want to start a task; it works great and motivates me to stop procrastinating.)* For example, if I'm stuck when trying to make a decision or feeling claustrophobic in a crowded elevator, I mentally say "5-4-3-2-1 GO!" and it spurs me to act. I may not be able to do more than shift my feet, but it's good practice to clear my mind and prepare me to take stronger action if I need to, if, for example, someone touches me inappropriately in the elevator and I need to confront them with a command to back off.

So, when you can, practice the countdown command to snap yourself into the present and take action. Or you can choose to think, as one woman did when two men tried to pull her into their car, "Fight now or die later!"

Fawning

Fawning is a behavior that may sound counter-intuitive, but for some victims—particularly those who were sexually, physically, or emotionally abused as children—it serves as a coping mechanism and way to protect themselves from further harm.

The dictionary defines fawning as "displaying exaggerated flattery or affection," in this case, by the victim toward the perpetrator. For example, when I was a child I was unable to fight or flee my abusers, so instead I went out of my way to reassure them that I liked them and that despite what they did to me, I thought they were good people. My goal was to show them I wasn't a threat, so they (hopefully) wouldn't hurt me. When they showed me any kind of affection or positive attention in return, I was flooded with relief and gratitude.

This is a form of Stockholm Syndrome, in which a victim is so terrorized that she becomes emotionally dependent on the moods and whims of her abuser. When any small kindness is extended by the abuser, the relief from the fear and terror is so great that the victim is suffused with gratitude and even love for the perpetrator. Of course, this is not real love; merely sheer relief that the harm has stopped, even if only for a short period.

Sadly, in retrospect, I can see that this made me an ideal victim because it tacitly encouraged the predators to continue abusing me without repercussion. Fawning became my *modus operandi* (MO), and I continued my fawning behavior well into adulthood because I continued to believe it would keep me safe. Obviously, it did not. It wasn't until I got into therapy in my early 30s that I was able to objectively see what I had been doing and release that behavior. My new MO is to call out potential threats early and often as they occur by, for example, telling creepy guys to respect my space.

The Potential Benefits of Fawning

All that being said, fawning can be a good tactic if you do it consciously, with the intention to throw the predator off his game. For example, you can appear to go along with the perpetrator's demands until an opportunity to flee or fight presents itself. Or you can appeal to his ego by saying something like, "I'm sure you're a good person; please don't hurt me." Again, you can appear to acquiesce until you find the right moment to change tactics if needed.

FLEEING

Your safest bet if you're confronted by a predator (and are physically able) is to run from the scene as fast as your legs can carry you. Yell at the top of your lungs and run toward locations with other people if you're near a populated area. Yelling is more powerful than screaming and more likely to cause you to verbalize your need for help. If you're in an isolated area or no one else is nearby, yell and run toward any lights you can see. Predators fear being caught and will often flee the scene themselves if their target is making loud noises and going toward a well-lit area.

For heaven's sake, do NOT yell "Fire!" to get people's attention. I know, you've been told that bystanders will react more positively than if you yell "Help," but If you yell "Fire," you waste precious time. After all, if someone calls the Fire Department, the firemen, when they arrive, will still have to call the police. Better to point to a specific person and yell, "Call 911!"

If you're confronted by someone who demands your purse or phone, do not HAND it to them! Instead, toss it to the ground as far away from you as possible and run. Chances are, they got what they wanted, and they'll go for the object and not pursue you further. Please, don't try to fight for your purse or phone. These can be replaced; your life can't.

If the attacker has a gun, run anyway (in a zig-zag pattern if you can, to make yourself a more difficult target). Your chances of being hit or seriously injured are relatively small. I read somewhere that there's a 98 percent chance the predator won't shoot, but if you go with him, there's a 98 percent chance you won't survive.[v]

If fleeing isn't physically possible, you may choose to fight the predator to save yourself from being injured, raped, killed, or taken to another location where you could be in even greater danger.

COMPLYING

Complying with the demands of a predator may be your safest option, depending on the situation and your assessment of your options. Following his demands is always a choice you can make, unless the predator wants to take you to another, secluded location (where you're much more likely to be severely wounded or killed), in which case your safest choice is to fight like hell for all you're worth.

Several studies have attempted to determine whether a person is better or worse off resisting in criminal situations, with varying and sometimes contradictory conclusions. My answer to that question is, *it depends*.

There are so many possible scenarios you could encounter and all involve multiple factors:

- Does the perpetrator just want your purse or is your very person being threatened?
- Are you being threatened with a weapon?
- Do *you* have a weapon or self-defense product?
- What is the location? Your home? A deserted alley? At a party?
- Is help nearby? Within yelling distance?
- Are you mentally prepared to seriously injure your attacker in order to escape?

At the moment a crime is taking place, you, better than anyone, are able to judge the situation and take action according to what you perceive to be in your best interest. Choosing not to resist is not wrong or shameful and neither is resistance. *The goal is your survival* and you should do whatever you feel you must to ensure the least amount of pain, suffering, debilitation, or death (to you).

Many U.S. states once had laws (a sad few still do) that state that if a victim doesn't fight back against an attacker with "vigor," it isn't considered rape. (Can you imagine? Now THAT is shameful on the part of legislators!) It's very easy after the fact to criticize others for their action or inaction, but we never know how we'll react until it happens to us. Don't let other people's opinions sway your decision either way.

Still, there are some facts you should be aware of that may influence your decision:

- 80 percent of the time, women took protective measures during rape attacks, including yelling and threatening, or attacking the perpetrator. In 60 percent of the attacks, their efforts enabled them to escape. For 7 percent, their actions didn't help them, and for 11 percent they made no difference.[vi]
- In 6 percent of cases, the perpetrators became more angry and aggressive, but the survivors were still able to avoid injury or greater injury.[vii]
- Only 26 percent of all violent crimes (assault, robbery, homicide, and sexual assault) were committed by offenders

armed with a weapon. About 10 percent involved the use of a gun. Attackers were armed in only 8 percent of rape cases.[viii]

- To commit the rape, most armed rapists will lay aside their weapons during the assault. This gives you a chance to fight back, using his own weapon against him, if necessary.
- When the perpetrators were not armed, the women most likely to be raped or harmed were those who didn't fight back.[ix]

When I was raped by the sheriff's deputy, I initially struggled, pleaded, and said no, but once I was overpowered, I dissociated and ceased fighting. I felt hopeless about my ability to get out of the rapist's control and, at some level, I decided I was safer not fighting back. For that, I blamed myself for decades.

Knowing what I know today about how to unleash my inner Tasmanian Devil to defend myself, I would now most likely fight back to avoid the rape. But I want you to know that that's a decision you, and only you, can make in the moment you're deciding how to respond. If you're afraid to fight or deem it unwise, then giving in to his demands may be your best option.

Even if you initially comply, the predator may still try to hurt or kill you, at which point, you can make the decision to change tactics and fight for your life. Remember, YOU are in control of your reactions. The most important thing is not to engage in the blame and shame game with yourself afterward. It's unproductive and emotionally devastating to carry shame for what HE did. Don't rent space in your head to any thoughts that make you into the bad guy. Just don't.

FIGHTING

I want you to imagine for a moment that you're walking to your car in a darkened garage. As you reach for the door handle, you hear footsteps behind you. Before you can turn around, a man shoves a gun in your back and demands you get in the car. When you hesitate, he threatens to kill you right there if you don't do what he says.

Do you resist? Yell? Fight him? Run away? (Hint: the answer to this question is almost always all the above.) If you resist and fight, you could be seriously injured or killed. But then, if you *don't* resist and fight, you're almost certain to be injured or killed.

One thing is for sure, if you do choose to resist and fight your attacker, you must do so with as much ferocity and ruthlessness as you can. That means yelling at the top of your lungs and biting, clawing, kicking, gouging, and punching every vulnerable point you can reach on the perpetrator's body.

Know that while you're defending yourself, the predator isn't just going to stand still and let you kick his butt around the block. He's likely going to fight you in return. I say this not to frighten you, but to prepare you for that fact. Fight through the pain anyway until you can escape.

Get angry. Get FURIOUS! After all, this person is trying to hurt or even kill you! Do whatever it takes to stop him. You don't owe it to him to be nice or polite. Unleash your inner Tasmanian Devil and fight as dirty as you possibly can! Don't stop just because you've put him on the ground. Make sure you've disabled him enough to convince him not to chase you when you flee.

When you encounter a predator, particularly when you're threatened with physical or sexual assault, you don't know how far things will go or what the perpetrator's intentions are—is he looking just to commit the assault and run off, or is he determined to kill any witnesses to the crime, including you? You may want to believe the perpetrator when he assures you that he won't harm you if you do what he says, but complying with his demands may be a bad idea.

Predators are incredible cowards; they choose victims based on whether they think they can control them. If you wear your confidence like a badge of honor, walking with your head up and being aware of your surroundings, you'll make predators think twice before choosing you as a target.

COMING UP NEXT...

In Chapter 3, I present common rape myths to illuminate the reality of the situation. Some of them are tricky and you may find you've been holding incorrect beliefs yourself. I'll talk about the characteristics of victims and predators, and provide facts about where and when most crimes occur. I'll also share interesting facts about the pros and cons of resisting an attacker.

Lies We Tell Ourselves

As a graduate student, I had to teach a class in a women's studies course for credit. I decided to conduct a study of rape myths and gave the entire class a simple quiz asking them to indicate whether they believed certain statements about rape and victims. About 30 percent of the class was male, so I figured I would get mixed results.

I was totally unprepared to find that nearly 75 percent of my classmates believed most of the myths, which included many of the ones listed below. Most surprising were the surveys that agreed with all the myths, indicating that either the test-takers were completely ignorant of the facts or simply messing with me. I wasn't sure which idea was more disturbing.

Myths and Facts about Rape

READ THROUGH THE popular myths and corresponding facts below and see if you find statements you thought were true. I hope these facts will illuminate your thinking.

Myth: *People are most often sexually assaulted by strangers.*

Fact: Approximately 82 percent of sexual assaults are perpetrated by people the survivors know, including 25 percent of sexual assaults, which are perpetrated by significant others.[x]

Myth: *I live in a safe community, so I don't have to worry about personal safety.*

Fact: Violence can occur anywhere, even in the nicest homes and on the safest campuses. In fact, half of all reported rape and sexual assault incidents occurred within a mile of the victims' homes or in their homes.[xi] I've met survivors who were assaulted in churches and others who were victimized in plain sight of others. Remaining vigilant in every environment is good practice and more likely to help you spot danger.

Myth: *If I look busy, they won't attack me.*

Fact: Being aware of your surroundings is crucial in determining whether you can avoid or escape an attack. Wearing headphones or earbuds, and playing with your phone are distractions that keep you from recognizing potential danger and make you an easy target. You're better off keeping your eyes on your surroundings and the people around you. Don't be afraid to make eye contact with others; it's one of the ways to "fail" the predator interview.

Myth: *I'll be able to tell if someone is dangerous by their appearance.*

Fact: Just because someone's wearing a black hoodie doesn't mean he's a criminal, just as someone wearing a suit isn't necessarily a good guy. Besides, most assaults are perpetrated by people we know.

Myth: If a woman drinks, wears revealing clothing, or walks alone at night, she's "asking for it."

Fact: The type of behavior a person engages in is irrelevant. You don't drink or dress up or walk alone because you're asking to be raped. What determines whether a rape occurs is the choice of the predator, not the victim.

Myth: Alcohol is a major cause of sexual assault in dating relationships.

Fact: Alcohol and drugs do not "cause" a perpetrator to commit sexual assault. But alcohol may be used as an excuse or justification for inappropriate or violent behavior, and may inhibit clear communication about sexual boundaries. A perpetrator may also use drugs or alcohol to overcome a woman's resistance by pressuring her to drink more or drugging her drink.[xii]

Myth: I'm safe from ingesting a date rape drug if I keep an eye on my drink to make sure no one tampers with it.

Fact: No one sits and stares at their drink without blinking, so someone can slip something into your beverage without you noticing. But while Rohypnol, or "roofies" as they're known on the street, are a concern you should be aware of, it's also the drink itself that could get you into trouble. When you drink too much, you hinder your ability to recognize threats before trouble occurs. Too many young college women (and men), away from home for the first time and eager to have fun, drink to excess and thereby become more vulnerable to sexual coercion. To make things worse, survivors who were drunk or had taken drugs around the time of the assault are less likely to report their victimization to authorities because they're afraid they'll be blamed or punished for their own behavior.

Myth: *College men who rape women are one-time offenders who just misinterpreted the situation or made a mistake.*

Fact: Not likely. According to research conducted by psychologist David Lisak, 90 percent of campus rapists are repeat offenders, averaging nearly six victims each. Lisak wrote, "They [predators] intentionally target women they perceive as vulnerable, often plying them with drugs or alcohol until their victims are too incapacitated to resist, and then sexually assault them. They count on the fact that sexual assault is perceived as a misunderstanding or drunken mistake. It is not."[xiii]

Myth: *Women often make up false accusations about being sexually assaulted to get attention, money, or revenge.*

Fact: Statistics on the number of false accusations dealing with sexual assault vary widely, but most studies agree that the number is between 2 and 8 percent, which is similar to other crimes. Overall, rape is an extremely underreported crime; it's estimated that about a third of sexual assaults are never reported.[xiv] (*Based on anecdotal evidence from the hundreds of women I've spoken to, I believe that number is much higher.*)

Myth: *I need to be in good shape to take a self-defense class.*

Fact: A proper self-defense class, focused on women and girls, will teach you techniques that target the attacker's weak spots, rather than requiring great strength or physical fitness on your part. I'm in my mid-50s and in just fair physical condition. I can't run 50 feet, but I feel confident about my ability to give a predator a run for his money using just the weapons my body offers.

Myth: *If someone's attacking me, I need to cause him pain in order to get away.*

Fact: The goal needs to be to injure and/or disable the perpetrator enough for you to escape, not just to cause him pain, which may merely infuriate him and cause you further injury.

Myth: *Pepper spray will stop an attacker.*

Fact: Pepper spray doesn't always work well, especially if you keep it buried in the bottom of your purse. *(You know who I'm talking to, ladies!)* If it's windy outside you could end up injuring yourself or the pepper spray container could be defective, wasting precious time when you could have been protecting yourself or running away. It can also be wrestled away from you and used to incapacitate you.

Myth: *If a perpetrator has a gun, do whatever he says.*

Fact: The odds of dying from a gunshot are very low. The perpetrator must actually fire the weapon, the bullet has to actually enter your body, and the bullet would have to do vital injury. The gun also must function, which, in almost half the cases, it won't because it is broken, unloaded, or fake.[xv] Overall, firearm assaults are lethal just 5.4 percent of the time.[xvi]

Myth: *Men commit rape because they need sexual satisfaction.*

Fact: There are a variety of reasons why predators rape others, unrelated to sexual satisfaction. Common reasons include control, revenge, a feeling of inferiority or superiority, disinhibition (under the influence of drugs or alcohol), and the desire to exert power over the victim.

Myth: *It's not rape if the victim doesn't fight back or try to get away.*

Fact: There's no right or wrong way to respond to rape. Whatever a person needs to do to survive the incident is the appropriate action for them. Many people go into shock and freeze during rape, but submission is NOT the same thing as consent.

Myth: *It's only rape if you're physically and violently sexually penetrated.*

Fact: Rape is rape if consent is not offered, even if the victim doesn't fight back or cry for help, or even if the assault doesn't involve physical violence. Non-consensual behavior, ranging from unwanted touching and groping, to full sexual penetration—involving any of the perpetrator's body parts (or other object) being forced on or into your body parts—is not only inappropriate, it's often against the law. While some jurisdictions require a verbal "No" be stated by you to the offender, other states, like California, now require you to affirm "Yes" to indicate consent. Every state has laws protecting victims who can't offer meaningful consent because of impairment by drugs, alcohol, or mental incapacitation.

Myth: *If you don't want to have sex, but give in because the man wears you down or you think he won't stop, it's still rape.*

Fact: This is a trick scenario. Unlike a situation in which you comply because a predator threatens, harms, or overpowers you (which is clearly rape), if you "give in" because you're tired of resisting, that is not, in fact, rape. Men are not psychic (as much as we wish they were). If you don't want to have sex with someone, even after you've engaged in heavy petting, you need to say so loud and clear, and give the man a chance to stop. Don't "suffer through it" and then later regret it and claim it was rape. This would not only be unfair, it would be a false claim and, thus, illegal.

Myth: *Once you've given consent, you can't take it back.*

Fact: This is not a trick. You *always* have the right to say "No" at *any* point during a sexual encounter and expect the other person to respect that. It doesn't matter whether you've had sex with that person before or if you intend to have sex with them again in the future (as might be the case in a partner relationship). No means no, and that applies to intimate partners as well as strangers.

Myth: *Men can't be raped.*

Fact: According to most statistics, 1 in every 33 men (or boys) experiences a rape or attempted rape, or other form of sexual violence, either by a woman (which occurs in nearly half the cases) or another man. These statistics are based on *reported* rapes and don't take into account those that go unreported. In a study on *Male Sexual Victimization: Examining Men's Experiences of Rape and Sexual Assault*, author Karen G. Weiss found that the prevalence of male rape is almost as common as that of women.[xvii] The U.S. Department of Justice's Bureau of Justice Statistics is also now including rapes that occur in prison settings in their reports, which is changing the view of rape as a problem faced almost exclusively by women and girls.

Myth: *After a victim suffers from a sexual assault incident, the worst is over.*

Fact: Sexual assault at any age can cause long-term damage including, but not limited to: post-traumatic stress disorder, depression, pregnancy, substance abuse, self-harm, suicide attempts, and sexually transmitted diseases.

Myth: *You should NEVER resist a criminal.*

Fact: Whether you choose to resist is entirely up to you and your best judgment, based on the circumstances. If all the perpetrator wants is your wallet or phone, throw them at a distance away from you and then run like the wind. Nothing on your phone is worth being injured or killed over.

Myth: *You should ALWAYS resist a criminal.*

Fact: This may be true if you feel you're in imminent physical danger. Again, your judgment of the situation will help you determine whether what the criminal wants is worth fighting for (if it's YOU, then it is). There are times when you must resist or be raped or killed, as in situations where the perpetrator wants to force you to go with him to a secondary location, like a car or alley.

How Effective is Resistance, Really?

Speaking of resistance, research conducted by Greg Ellifritz reveals that:[xviii]

- Victims who cried or pleaded with the perpetrator without offering any resistance were raped 96 percent of the time.
- Those who screamed were victimized between 44 and 50 percent of the time.
- Those who ran were raped 15 percent of the time.
- Those who forcefully resisted (without a weapon) were raped 14 percent of the time.

- Those who resisted with knives or guns of their own were raped less than 1 percent of the time.
- Resistance only hurt their situations about 9 percent of the time.

Characteristics of Victims and Predators

While there are no typical victims or perpetrators of violence, there are trends. For example:

- Targets of sexual assault tend to be young; more than half of survivors report their first rape occurred before they were 18. Thirty percent of female rape survivors were between 18 and 24.[xix]
- Some predators select their victims because they have specific characteristics, for example, a certain hair color, body size, ethnicity, profession, or physical appearance that may be like someone else they know.[xx]
- People who are physically or sexually abused as children are twice as likely to be raped later in life than those who are not abused.[xxi]

It seems obvious that most predators who target women have negative or conflicting attitudes about them. Again, no two predators are alike, but research shows:

- Studies of incarcerated rapists indicate that younger men generally commit sexual assaults against strangers.[xxii]

- While they may have difficulty maintaining adult relationships, predators usually have access to consensual sexual partners, but still choose to commit rape.[xxiii]
- Sexual offenders often exhibit a sense of entitlement, a need for power and control, hostility and anger, and acceptance of interpersonal violence of all kinds.[xxiv]
- Many incarcerated rapists have had at least one prior conviction (most often for violent crimes, burglaries, or theft).[xxv]
- Predators convicted of sexual offenses are more likely than other offenders to commit additional sexual crimes.[xxvi]
- The average age of a rapist is 31 years old.[xxvii]
- 52 percent of rapists are white.[xxviii]
- 22 percent of imprisoned rapists are married.[xxix]
- In one-third of sexual assaults, the criminal is intoxicated with alcohol; 4 percent of them are on drugs.[xxx]
- Rapists are more likely to be serial criminals than serial rapists (in other words, they're looking for crimes of opportunity).
- Predators are more likely to attack a woman walking by herself who is not aware of her surroundings (e.g., using her cell phone).

Where and When Crimes Tend to Occur

- The greatest number of rapes occur in cities outside major metropolitan areas (the suburbs). The fewest occur in rural areas.[xxxi]
- 36 percent of sexual assaults and 13 percent of rapes occur in public places, such as parks, deserted streets, public buildings, and bars and nightclubs.[xxxii]

- A study of convicted rapists found that most committed their crimes near their current or previous homes.[xxxiii]
- 4 in 10 crimes take place in the victims' homes. 20 percent take place in the home of a friend, neighbor, or relative. 1 in 12 takes place in a parking garage.[xxxiv]
- 24 percent take place between midnight and 6 a.m.[xxxv]

COMING UP NEXT...

In the next chapter, I'll define intuition and situational awareness, and discuss their importance in keeping you safe. Intuition is your greatest weapon, providing advance warning of potential danger so you can thwart an attack. I'll also share three "things your mother didn't teach you," and talk about boundaries and how to defend them.

CHAPTER 4

Intuition: Learning to Trust Your Gut

Shont'e was carrying her groceries home after a long day. When she got into the elevator there was a man she vaguely recognized as a resident of the building. When he saw her shift one of the bags in her arms, he said, "Hey, let me carry those for you," and reached to take them from her.

Shont'e felt uneasy and said, "No, that's okay. I've got it." The man frowned and said aggressively, "What? I'm not good enough to carry your groceries?" Shont'e was shocked; she hadn't meant to offend him and now felt badly for being rude. She reluctantly handed over the grocery bags and they went the rest of the way to her floor in awkward silence.

When she got to her door, Shont'e reached out to take her bags back. The man said, "No, I'll take them in for you." At that point, her gut was screaming at her to get away from this person. But he pushed past her into the apartment and before Shont'e had time to react, she found herself in a struggle with the man and was raped. After threatening to kill her if she told anyone, the man left Shont'e bruised and shocked on the floor.

"All I could think then was how stupid, stupid, stupid I was to let that man into my apartment," Shont'e said. "I knew before I handed over my bags that something wasn't right, but I was afraid of offending him, so I let him take over the whole situation. I never reported him because of his threat and because I was so ashamed and humiliated."

How We Lose Touch with Our Intuition

WE ALL HAVE intuition. We were born with it. The only way we "lose" it is if it's socialized out of us by repeated instructions or victimizations that cause us to doubt or purposely silence it. Well-intentioned parents teach us to ignore that important voice within that tells us when something isn't right because they want us to be polite and accepted by others.

For those who were sexually, physically, or emotionally abused as children, you quickly learned that internal voice simply complicated things. After all, what good is your intuition if you can never act on it because you're vulnerable and small? When you're repeatedly victimized, you learn to distrust your intuition and believe it to be faulty.

It is my strong personal belief that the majority of rapes occur because the victims don't want to be rude. In uncomfortable or ambiguous situations, they override their intuition and don't stand up for their boundaries, making them so, so vulnerable.

If you're a woman, chances are you don't trust your intuition and may even actively ignore it, or worse, act counter to it. In my lifetime, I can't count the number of times when my gut was screaming at me and I chose to proceed anyway, with unfortunate results.

In his bestselling book, *The Gift of Fear,* author Gavin de Becker observes that while many people initially claim their victimizing event happened "out of the blue," when prompted to recite the details they begin to recall tiny facts and moments that troubled them at the time. "The guy was wearing sneakers with his suit instead of dress shoes," or "Something about the way she smiled told me she couldn't be trusted."

But many times, our guts react with no discernable cues. At the time of my first sexual assault at 19, I was taken totally by surprise, but looking back I remember I felt really uncomfortable going into the man's apartment. Why would my gut clench just walking into his place? After all, he hadn't said or done anything up to that point (that I can recall) that would have led me to suspect him.

I now believe my intuition picked up on subtle changes in his energy and facial expression. If I'd been aware of and trusted my intuition, I wouldn't have entered that man's apartment and likely wouldn't have been assaulted that night *(again, not my fault—he chose to rape me)*. And if I had trusted myself as I do now, today, I wouldn't have gone out with him in the first place.

Signature Signs of Intuition

Your body is a finely tuned instrument of wisdom and knowing. It's constantly giving you cues about your environment and the people in it.

Some of these cues include:

- A feeling of wariness or foreboding.
- The hair on the back of your neck and arms may stand up, just as it does in animals who sense something threatening in their environment.
- A sick or sinking feeling in the stomach.
- Shortened, shallow breathing.
- Pounding heart.
- A rise in blood pressure.
- A rush of adrenaline.
- Tunnel vision.
- Difficulty hearing.
- Feelings of panic or anxiety.

When we feel threatened, our bodies go into a heightened response mode. Your brain produces large amounts of adrenaline (the hormone epinephrine) and releases it into the bloodstream, along with dopamine and norepinephrine, all stress chemicals designed to prepare the body to go into fight or flight mode.

Your heart begins to beat harder and faster to give your vital organs the extra oxygen they need to function optimally. Your pupils dilate to allow more light to enter, while at the same time they achieve greater focus by excluding objects in your peripheral vision (called tunnel vision). Your ears do something similar, so you hear some things more clearly, while other sounds may be muted. Your body produces extra glucose for energy to help you when you fight or flee.

This chemical soup causes the sensations listed above and more. You *must* learn to trust that when these sensations appear, something isn't right in your environment and you need to act NOW to remove yourself from the situation. That may mean excusing yourself to use the ladies room on a date and sneaking out the back door to escape, or it may mean forcefully telling someone to back off. In Shont'e's case, it may have meant handing over the groceries to the creepy neighbor and then running like hell for help before they ever went upstairs, leaving him, literally, holding the bag. Do whatever it takes to honor your intuition and protect yourself.

The Importance of Situational Awareness

I have the worst situational awareness on the planet. No, really, I mean it. My husband once shaved his beard and I didn't notice it until he pointed it out at the end of the day. My lack of mindfulness is largely because I'm so task-oriented that when I'm focused on something, I'm oblivious to everything happening around me. I'm also really good at dissociating (checking out mentally), a carry-over from my victim days.

And this is a very bad thing, for several reasons I'll cover below. In a nutshell, situational awareness means you know what's going on around you. Not having it means you're clueless and a bullseye for criminals.

Predators are generally opportunistic; they tend to look for victims they consider easy marks, and many crimes are crimes of opportunity, meaning perpetrators seize the chance to rob or assault someone because the opportunity is there and there's a good chance they won't be caught.

As women, we're automatically considered to be vulnerable targets by criminals who are physically stronger and more intimidating. Plus, we often aren't paying attention to what's going on around us, focusing instead on our smart phones or fishing in our handbag for our car keys (our fingers slipping right over the mace sitting at the bottom on the purse), making us the perfect victims for opportunistic predators.

I was raised with the idea that it's best to avoid eye contact with people and later heard that if you're on your cell phone, criminals are less likely to attack you because someone is listening. These are myths, and dangerous ones at that. Avoiding eye contact can make you appear afraid and less likely to resist a perpetrator, and talking on your phone makes you more vulnerable, not less, because, you guessed it, you're not being situationally aware.

Awareness of your environment and the people around you is a necessary skill you must practice to become proficient. Your awareness feeds your gut information it needs to decide whether you're safe or not. When your intuition is triggered, you need to laser focus on what the problem is. If you can't discern any obvious reason for your gut reaction, trust it anyway and remove yourself from the situation.

A friend of mine took a class that included practicing wide-angle vision, which involved sitting for five to 10 minutes a day in a state of present awareness. She was instructed to notice what was going on around her, so while staring ahead, she noticed the red flash of a cardinal landing on the branch of a nearby tree, the wasp in the corner of the eave, the sound of the crows cawing from behind her house. This type of awareness training has been practiced by indigenous tribes for thousands of years. Today, the busy-ness of our lives and the technology around us have decreased our situational awareness—a skill we need to practice if we're to enjoy the present moment and know what's going on in our environment.

Acting on Your Intuition

Don't, I repeat—do NOT give someone the benefit of the doubt if you feel uncomfortable around them. Challenge them in whatever way is appropriate at that moment. Whether it's staring them hard in the eyes, telling them to back off, or yelling for help, you decide what's necessary.

Don't be afraid of being wrong or looking silly. When you tell someone to back off and give you space, if he's a good guy he'll do it and likely apologize. If he's a predator, he'll get angry with you and try to make you feel badly about confronting him. This is your clue that he's not to be trusted. While nothing may come of it, you might actually have thwarted an attack against you.

A QUICK HUDDLE

Let me just stop here for a moment and address those of my readers who are right now thinking, "But that would be rude!" or "I couldn't possibly call someone out like that—I'm too nice/polite/timid/afraid/insert your own objection here."

Ladies, we have GOT to get over this outdated and outright dangerous kind of thinking if we're going to make it through this life with any sense of security and sanity. Tell that voice in your head to *shut the hell up.* It's harming you; it's harming us all by perpetuating the false belief that we, as women, don't have the ability or right to protect the integrity of our bodies, minds, and spirits.

I'm sick to say that nearly 100 percent of the women I've met as I've spoken around the country have admitted to experiencing some form of sexual behavior that made them uncomfortable or afraid. They got creepy phone calls late in the night with heavy breathing on the other end of the line. They were harassed by rangy herds of young men who followed them halfway home while they tried not to cry. They were felt up on the bus by strangers. Their uncles drunkenly French kissed them when they were just getting used to their training bras. They were drugged and raped at a frat party. They were kidnapped and repeatedly assaulted.

I've also had women come up and proudly tell me they've never experienced any kind of assault, adding "Of course there was that one time when my friend's father..."

And most of these women blamed themselves, some so harshly that, like me, they played judge and jury—sentencing themselves to life in emotional prison *for something that wasn't even their fault!*

Aren't you *sick* of living like this? Aren't you tired of feeling afraid every time you walk by yourself through a dark, deserted parking lot? Tired of scurrying with your keys clenched in your fist until you can breathlessly throw yourself into the driver's seat and slam down the door lock? Tired of not feeling safe to move around the world in peace and security?

If you ARE sick and tired of living a life dominated by fear and hypervigilance, then you *must* reject the idea that you're not worth fighting for, and claim your right to feel safe and secure! You simply *must* step into your power and take action on your own behalf to protect yourself when you feel threatened.

Before you agree to that first (or second) date or before you go to that location that makes your gut clench, THINK about what you're doing. Check in with your intuition and your body to get their opinions first. You don't owe it to anyone to do what they want, even if they're persistent (and bad guys will be persistent). If you want to do whatever it is you're considering and it aligns with your intuition and integrity, do it. If it doesn't resonate with you and you have doubts, don't do it. It's that simple.

The more in tune you are with your inner voice, the more quickly you'll recognize and listen to it when you need it. When it tells you to be careful, to do something different, heed that voice! It's your best friend and it won't steer you wrong.

Trust your gut and your body, and then ACT! If you respond to defend yourself from a threatening person—whether it's verbally or physically, or even by just removing yourself from the situation—you send a signal that it's *not* okay for the perpetrator to escalate his advances. Be as polite or rude as needed to maintain your boundaries and your safety.

Think about it for a second. In fact, take 15 seconds. Seriously, take the next 15 seconds and just sit there and breathe. It didn't last long, did it? THAT's about how long your embarrassment will last when you set a clear boundary with someone.

15 seconds. Isn't the discomfort you and they might feel worth not getting raped? Isn't it worth it to avoid a lifetime of post-traumatic stress? Of course it's worth it! *So DO it*. Be embarrassed; you'll live through it and so will the other person.

Badass Tip

If you're in a tough spot where your intuition is blaring and you feel frozen with indecision about how to respond, ask yourself the following questions:

- Would I be proud to tell my daughter/granddaughter/niece/mother/best friend how I handled this situation?
- If my daughter/granddaughter/niece/mother/best friend were in this same situation, would I want them to respond the same way I'm currently doing?

If you say "No" to either question, then you need to stop and rethink your options. Change tactics and behave in a manner you would be proud for your loved ones to witness.

"No" is a Complete Sentence

My stepdaughter taught me one of the most important lessons of my life. While visiting me at office at the North Carolina Attorney General's Office one day back in 1998, I took Amy, then 8, into the cafeteria, which was managed by a nice blind gentleman named Eddie.

When we got to the counter with our sodas, Eddie said, "You sound like a sweetie-pie. Come give Eddie a hug." Amy quietly but firmly said, "No, thank you."

I was horrified! I was afraid she had embarrassed poor Eddie and started to scold her. Then I stopped and thought about it for a moment, and realized she was right to refuse to hug a strange man. I was totally awed by her ability to protect herself so neatly and politely, and in a way that until that day, I was not able to do. I was never more proud of her.

Since that time, I never encourage children (including my own grandchildren) to hug or kiss me or any other person unless they want to—and chances are, if the person is a stranger, they don't want to.

Things Your Mother Didn't Teach You

- You can say "NO" in ANY situation where you feel uncomfortable.
- It's okay to be rude. Sometimes politeness doesn't work and you simply have to be more forceful. There may even be times when you need to be just plain rude to a persistent person who's invading your personal space. I used to think

that women who were rude to guys who hit on them were just bitchy, but came to appreciate that sometimes that's the only way to get the message across.

- You can save yourself! You're not a princess and there's no knight in shining armor waiting in the wings to rescue you. You're a strong, intelligent person who is perfectly capable of defending your own boundaries.

Putting Your Boundaries to the Test

Boundaries represent the line you allow people to cross (or not) in your physical and emotional space. We set them up to protect us from intrusion by other people. Healthy boundaries look like a circle, with you in the middle (as the person you most trust), surrounded by a larger circle that you save for your closest friends and loved ones, and then outer circles for acquaintances, and finally, for people you don't know or don't trust.

Unhealthy boundaries are vague and, in some cases, may be totally missing in action. This is often the case for those who've been victimized by people they should have been able to trust. When someone is abused by a trusted caregiver, their boundaries become confused, leading them to either not trust anyone or to allow anyone trample them.

Predators will test your boundaries to determine whether you'll make a good victim. They often first attempt to cross your emotional boundaries by making suggestive or inappropriate comments or jokes to see how you react. If you make it clear they've crossed a line, they'll usually back off. If you giggle nervously or "make nice," they'll push further in an attempt to manipulate you into a bad situation.

If someone crosses a physical or emotional boundary with you, you *must* let them know right away, whether it's a stranger or someone you know well. A simple, "I'm not comfortable with that," may be all it takes. Sure, you may both feel uncomfortable for a few moments after you set a firm boundary, but isn't your body, your very life worth that small and passing discomfort?

This can be hard to do with people you know and like; in fact, it takes courage to stand in your integrity. But it's really important to stick to your guns. If the person is genuinely decent, they may be a bit put off, but they'll stop the offending behavior. If they don't, you know you're dealing with someone who's trying to control or manipulate you, and you need to get away from them as quickly as possible.

Here are some polite but firm responses to boundary violations:

- "Sorry, but I'm not comfortable with you standing so close. Could you please move back a bit?"
- "Excuse me, but that's not okay with me."
- "I don't agree with that (statement)."
- "It bothers me that you would say that."
- "I'm not open to that."
- "NO." (Enough said.)

Anytime someone willfully crosses your boundaries, you should take it very seriously. Be as passionate about protecting yourself as you would be for someone you love. *(We're all guilty of what I call "Dear Abby Syndrome," in which we feel free to tell our friends how to take care of themselves while blithely ignoring our own advice. Stop it.)* If you don't defend your boundaries, the situation could escalate into a verbal or physical attack.

Here's something you may not know—you can say no at any point in an encounter with someone, even a hot and heavy sexual encounter. It's entirely up to you to decide how far things should go. If what's happening in your interaction with another person isn't 100 percent okay with you, then it's perfectly acceptable to say "No," "Not now," or "Not yet."

It's okay to take a moment to check in with yourself. When you consult your head, your heart, and your gut, you'll know what to do.

COMING UP NEXT...

In Chapter 5, I'll expose the fact that, contrary to popular belief, most assaults are committed by people we know, not strangers. I'll also touch on partner violence and stalking behaviors so you can recognize when you're in a dangerous situation that might require outside support to disengage from. Then I'll share tips to help you stay safe when you're dealing with strangers in the online dating world.

Knowing Who You're Dealing With

Carrie, 16, was devastated when her older friend Lanie died. It was the first time she'd experienced the death of someone close to her. At the family gathering after the funeral, the adults broke out the liquor and the devastated husband drank too much. At one point, Carrie walked by the recliner he was sitting in and he pulled her onto his lap. She could immediately feel his erection as he rubbed against her, murmuring drunkenly about what a hot body she had.

Carrie was horrified! She looked frantically around the room and caught the eye of another adult, who quickly looked away in embarrassment. She had no idea what to do; she didn't want to humiliate the man in front of the whole family by making a scene, and besides, he was drunk and grieving, so he obviously wasn't in control of himself. Carrie desperately wanted him to stop and finally pulled out of his grip and ran into another room. She was too embarrassed for them both to tell her parents and she wasn't convinced she would be believed if she did.

Acquaintance Assaults

WHEN PEOPLE THINK about predators, especially rapists, they imagine a stranger in a dark alley, but 82 percent of reported rapes are committed by someone we know—friends or acquaintances (38 percent); intimate partners (28 percent); and others, such as colleagues, neighbors, or people you've met but don't know well.[xxxvi]

Laws in most states generally don't distinguish between assaults committed by strangers and ones committed by people known to the victim. But sadly, date and acquaintance rapes are prosecuted less frequently and punished less severely than stranger rapes. Cases involving acquaintance rapes are more likely to go unreported or be withdrawn before prosecution, are more likely to be challenged in court by the perpetrator, and are the least likely to end in a conviction of the assailant.

This is partly due to traditional gender roles we've been socialized to accept, such as the idea that women should be passive in romantic and sexual relationships. Some people believe women say no to sexual advances only because they're expected to put up some resistance when, really, they "want it." Some men don't perceive themselves as rapists, believing that women are just playing hard to get and really want to be overpowered, and they would be shocked if they were accused of rape.

So, what's a guy to think? Well, men need to be sensitive to ANY signs of resistance and respect them. If they're unsure whether the person they're with is open to engaging in sex, they should simply ask their partner to provide a clear "Yes" if she's willing. If she says no, then sex is off the table, at least at that moment (the woman may choose differently later, again by offering a clear "Yes").

In a perfect world, more men would respect women and their right to rule their bodies at all times. Many great organizations are working to educate men in this regard, but we still have a long, long way to go.

Partner Violence

No matter how hard you try, you can't love someone out of hurting you—*because their behavior is not about you!* It's not. It's about their inner demons, and their capacity and willingness to project them onto you.

Intimate partner violence covers a broad range of behaviors:

- Emotional abuse, which includes verbal assaults, insults, and name-calling.
- Being jealous or possessive.
- Controlling how and where you spend your money, or not allowing you to have any money (to exert economic control so you can't afford to leave him).
- Threatening you with violence or weapons.
- Harming or threatening to harm your children or pets.

- Hurting you by kicking, shoving, slapping, choking, hitting, or punching you.
- Blaming you for his own violent acts.
- Forcing you to engage in sexual acts.
- Keeping you from going about your normal life, such as going to school or work, or seeing your friends and family.

Never announce your intention to leave your abuser in advance or he may try to forcibly keep you from leaving. And don't use it as a threat in the hope he'll stop the abuse, because it could make him more violent. Quietly make arrangements to leave when he isn't present, keeping a suitcase with your clothing, cash and credit cards, and important documents in a safe location so you can leave at a moment's notice. Enlist the help of your local domestic violence shelter for advice and protection if you need it.

When you leave, make it permanent. You must cut off all contact, because if you go back, and I've seen this a hundred times, things may be better for a short time, but he will again become abusive and you might not be able to get away this time. Use the caller ID on your phone and *never* answer his calls; block his number and "unfriend" him from your social media sites so you don't have to see his threats or pleas. Don't try to explain why you're ending the relationship; just let it be over and done.

Stalking

Some abusers simply can't let go and begin stalking their former intimate partners, closely monitoring what they do and where they go, looking for the right time to strike or trying to convince them to come back.

Stalking is much more common than people realize:

- In the U.S., an estimated 15.2 percent of women have experienced stalking during their lifetimes that made them feel very fearful, or made them believe that they or someone close to them would be harmed or killed.[xxxvii]
- 62 percent of female survivors were approached at home or work by their stalker. Over half received unwanted text or voice messages. Nearly half were watched, followed, or spied on with a listening device, camera, or GPS device.[xxxviii]
- Among female stalking victims, an estimated 88 percent were stalked by male perpetrators. Among male stalking victims, over half were stalked by female perpetrators.[xxxix]
- Both male and female victims often identified their stalkers as people they knew or with whom they at one time had an intimate relationship. Among female stalking victims, nearly 61 percent were stalked by a current or former intimate partner, nearly 25 percent were stalked by an acquaintance, 16 percent were stalked by a stranger, and about 6 percent were stalked by a family member.[xl]

When You *Don't* Know Them

Many people strictly envision sexual predators as strangers lurking in the bushes in a park waiting to lunge at passing joggers. Another reason many people believe that most assaults are perpetrated by strangers is because they hear on the news about online dates gone bad.

Below, I'll share some tips, many that my sister Susan Gray came up with, based on her personal experience as a divorced woman actively engaged in the online dating scene.

GOOD ADVICE TO AVOID BAD DATES

When looking at cars or other big purchases, you do a lot of online research, right? You want to make sure you get what you want at a price you can afford, so you check out every review you can find about that item.

If you found out a particular car had been in three prior accidents or failed the crash safety test, would you still consider it? Of course not! You need to show that same level of care and concern when engaging in online dating.

Without looking like a stalker, you can do some research before that first date. Get the person's last name and see if they have a Facebook page or other social media profiles. Looking through someone's photos and posts can tell you a lot about their personality. Also, do a simple Google search on their name and see what comes up.

You can also check to see if their profile photo is legitimately theirs by looking for it on a site called www.TinEye.com. (Right click on their profile photo and paste it to your desktop, then go to TinEye.com and choose the photo on your desktop; hit submit.) Many scammers, also called "catfishers," use photos of other people they found on the web for their profiles. If TinEye finds their image and it doesn't point back to that person, you know you're dealing with a scammer. End all communications with them immediately.

There are also websites that charge a nominal fee for a single background check, or a monthly fee where you can conduct as many searches as you like. These sites provide you with a wealth of information, from the subject's address and employer, to any arrest record they might have. Yes, there's a cost involved, but isn't your safety and well-being worth $25 a month?

You Hold the Cards.

It's your date, and if you plan wisely, you hold the majority of the cards. Before you go out, agree on what you're both expecting from the date. A short first date for a drink or cup of coffee is just fine, so don't feel pressured to meet before you're ready or for any longer than you're comfortable with.

If you so choose, make it abundantly clear that there will be no sex on the first date (or second, or whatever. YOU are in charge!). Too many men trolling online dating sites assume that if they buy you dinner, you "owe" them. If they know without a doubt sex is off the table, they'll either proceed with the plans, or disappear. If they disappear, they weren't worth dating anyway.

Stay in Public.

The safest plan is to meet somewhere public and stay somewhere public. Make your own way there and back, and don't feel pressured to go home with your date. Seriously, don't be pressured into doing anything you're not totally comfortable with. If he continues to insist that you go home with him (or to your place) despite your wishes otherwise, firmly tell him no and don't see him again. If you do feel ready to move to a private environment, make sure your expectations match his so there's no confusion about what he's expecting.

LEAVE BREADCRUMBS

Always text a friend or family member about your plans. In the text, say what time and where you're meeting, your date's full name and phone number, and your plans for the evening. If any of your plans change, update your contact through another text.

It's also a smart idea to text your loved one when you're on your way home and when you expect to arrive there. That way, you leave "breadcrumbs" (bits of information on your whereabouts) that can be used to find you in the event you don't show up when and where you're supposed to.

GET TO KNOW THE PERSON, NOT THE PROFILE

We all know people aren't necessarily the most honest in their online profiles, and how people interact online isn't always the same when you're face-to-face. You may have great interactions and banter with someone online, but then when you meet him in person, he's about as exciting as a box of rocks.

Don't be offended if your date is more guarded when meeting in person or if things don't progress as quickly face-to-face. You should be guarded as well. Refrain from giving out too much personal information, like your address, until you feel more comfortable with him.

If *any* alarm bells go off in your head or gut (if, for example, he makes inappropriate comments or jokes, or exhibits a sense of entitlement or an attitude towards women that's unsettling), it's perfectly okay to end the date early. You can do it up front, by saying something like "I'm not really feeling a connection, but it was great to meet you. I'm going home now." Or you can lie, saying something like "My dog/cat/guinea pig has been sick, and I really need to go home to check on him." If you're really concerned about the person, you could excuse yourself to go to the restroom and then just leave and go home. Doing what you feel you need to do to stay safe is always okay, even if others may consider it "rude."

TAKE SOME FORM OF PROTECTION

I don't necessarily mean condoms (although you should always have those in your purse just in case). Personal protection comes in many forms. For some, it's taking a self-defense class; while for others it means carrying a firearm, mace, a stun gun, or other personal security device. I can't encourage you strongly enough to purchase at least one highly-rated self-defense device that you keep readily at hand (not in the bottom of your purse!) in the event you need it. *(There are many new products on the market that I'll be reviewing on my website (www.cjscarlet.com) for you to check out.)*

If you find yourself saying NO repeatedly, and your date won't stop and you honestly feel you're in danger, try telling him that you need to get your "protection" from your car or purse. He doesn't need to know that it's a can of mace or a gun. If you excuse yourself to go to your car to get your "protection," just leave and get to a safe place right away.

First Date Clues He's Not a Good Guy

Many folks would be surprised to know that on a date, people will generally tell you who they really are. On one first date, the guy I was with told me that his ex-wife thought he was a moody slob. Typical of my desire to be liked and to make people feel good about themselves, I rushed to assure him I thought this wasn't really true, and for the first month I saw no signs of that kind of behavior. Sure enough, though, over time I learned he was both moody and very much a slob.

On your first or second date, when the conversation turns to past relationships, try asking: "What kinds of things does your ex (spouse/girlfriend) say about you?" or, "What would your ex say is the reason you guys split up?" You'd be surprised how readily most people will answer this question honestly; they're usually eager to go into detail of how that "bitch/bastard" hosed them over. This information can provide important clues into their thinking and behavior. Pay attention!

When he answers the first question ("What kinds of things does your ex say about you?"), take that information VERY seriously. If he says, "My ex claims I abused her/her child/her dog," it's possible he may have been falsely accused, but it's also possible he actually did what he was accused of. You need to be on your strictest guard for other indications that he has anger issues or a bad attitude toward women. Know that he may not reveal his temper initially, during the romancing phase, and be alert to subtle cues, like a tendency toward jealousy. If he talks badly about others and seems to think every other guy is a "jerk" and half the women are "bitches," you may be dealing with an abusive person or a narcissist. Get out of the relationship immediately!

The dynamics of why we choose the relationships we do is too complex to go into in this book. Just pay attention to the things your date says and does, and the way he treats you and you'll find clues about his future behavior. In my case, my date in 1980 gave me clues that trouble might be afoot. The man was overbearing and assumptive—ordering my food for me at a restaurant without asking me what I wanted, and sharing life experiences in a way that revealed anger issues and a sense of entitlement.

Most guys are good, decent, respectable human beings who would never harm a hair on your head; others are looking for any opportunity to victimize you. The problem is, it's not always easy to tell which is which. Check in regularly with your gut and remain open but cautious until you can definitively put him in the "good guy" category.

Do your homework and invest in your personal protection!

Coming Up Next...

Chapter 6 is packed with critically important facts about the characteristics and mindset of predators, as well as descriptions of the different types of predators you might encounter. You'll learn what predators want and what they DON'T want you to know. When you're done with this chapter, you'll have a greater understanding of the predatory mind and be better equipped to avoid dangerous encounters.

CHAPTER 6

What Predators *Don't* Want You to Know

The six of us, each from different criminal justice agencies, chatted amiably as we waited for Charles to join us. As he entered the room, we shifted nervously in our seats. Charles was a convicted child molester who was finishing up an offender treatment program and would soon be back on the street.

It was downright creepy the way he calmly answered our questions about how he selected his victims. "First I look for kids who are lonely or different; the ones who clearly need a friend. I start out asking them questions about what they like, what their favorite games are, which superhero they like the most. They're so eager for attention that they'll do almost anything for it."

He continued, "Once they like me and trust me, that's when I know I've got them. At that point, I could do anything to them and they won't even protest. I threaten them not to tell, but it's hardly even necessary. They're just so hungry for the attention. It's adorable."

It was sickening to listen to Charles talk about these children as if they were his puppets. We shifted the conversation to the offender treatment program and how well it was working. Charles clearly was telling us what we wanted to hear—that the program was working and he felt rehabilitated.

But our last question revealed his true nature when an assistant district attorney asked, "When you get out, will you do it again?"

Charles looked down and was silent for a full minute. When he lifted his head, his expression was sly and defiant. "Absolutely."

I shivered with dread and fury. Charles was to be released the next week, having served his sentence, and there wasn't a damned thing we could do about it.

Who the Predators Are

PREDATORS *REALLY* DON'T want you to read this chapter. It's your resource for information about who they are, how they select and groom their victims, and things they hope you won't do to protect yourself.

There are several types of predators out there, some of whom cross into more than one category:

- **The opportunistic predator** is looking for any chance that presents itself to commit a crime. If he sees you on your phone, dangling your handbag, he may run up from behind and snatch your purse. If he sees a couple out late at night on a deserted street, he may rob them at knife or gunpoint. If he sees you jogging alone at night, he may attempt to rape you. The type of crime doesn't matter as much as the payoff. Chances are, the predator is a stranger who puts little thought into his crimes and jumps you out of nowhere.
- **The "good" guy** may appear to be an upstanding citizen in all other aspects of his life, but he'll take advantage of a situation to commit what he may or may not perceive to be a crime. The best example of this is a college student who rapes an acquaintance at a party, especially if drugs or alcohol are involved that disinhibit his and her actions. This may actually be his *modus operandi*, drinking too much and then later claiming he was too impaired to know what he was doing if confronted later on. He may

intentionally take advantage of a woman who herself is impaired by drugs or alcohol, or he may misread the situation and go too far with his advances. It doesn't matter how good or nice he normally is, this kind of behavior is criminal and should be reported.

- **The stalker** is often a mentally unbalanced person who doesn't recognize personal boundaries and feels entitled to invade your life to get what he wants—your attention. He sometimes has a personal relationship with you, but not always. Usually, you're aware of and feel threatened by him, and may choose to report his behavior to the police.

- **The bully** is usually triggered by challenges to his masculinity or authority. If you embarrass him in front of his friends, he's likely to threaten or attack you to protect his image. Many batterers fall into this category.

- **The molester** grooms his victims, child or adult, to find the ones who will put up the least resistance, and he's highly skilled at testing the circumstances. He's also proficient at living a dual role in life, one that many outsiders may see as normal. He finds ways to put himself in situations where he has access to potential victims. He may be hard to spot, especially for children who tend to trust and obey adults.

- **The sociopathic predator** is a very dangerous character. While he may be very charismatic, he has no conscience, and no empathy or compassion for his victims. He's ruthless in his attempts to get what he wants, and trying to reason with him is useless; he simply doesn't care how his actions impact you and he has no remorse for his crimes.

What Predators Really Want

Bottom line: Predators have only one interest—to satisfy their own needs for power, control, or sexual satisfaction. They enjoy their victims' response to the acts as much as the acts themselves. They're seeking victims who respond as they desire—either by fighting, which allows the predators to overpower them, or by complying, which may motivate the predators to complete their crimes with no resistance. Above all, they want victims who won't report the crime. It's that simple.

When a man attacks a woman, it's usually about control—of her behavior, body, emotions, boundaries, or money. Predators will usually begin by taking control of little things, such as running the conversation or telling inappropriate jokes to gauge your reaction and, if you don't object, they'll move on to increasingly invasive behavior. Their actions could escalate quickly and start out with the predator violating your personal space or cornering you in an isolated location. They have one goal, to perpetrate their crime.

Predators are also on the lookout for the means to commit their crimes. They may watch you closely for a period of time, from minutes to months. They may seek out weapons they can use to threaten you. They're always looking for the best locations to position you that offer the greatest secrecy and ability to flee quickly and easily. They're counting on you to be terrified and compliant.

What Predators *Don't* Want

The number one thing predators don't want is to get caught, especially if they plan to use a weapon, which results in longer prison sentences if they're convicted. This is their biggest fear. Use it against them!

Predators are more likely to be put off when you:

- Walk confidently and with purpose. Take up as much space as possible; hold your chin up and stand tall. This makes you appear stronger and more likely to resist a predator.
- Pay attention to where you are and what's going on around you. Talking or playing on your cell phone makes you more, not less, vulnerable. Although talking to your friend or parent on your cell phone when you're walking the quad may make you feel safer, it actually puts you at greater risk of being attacked. And really, what are your friend or parents supposed to do if, in fact, you're attacked while you're talking to them? They're basically helpless and can't even call police if they're not in the same 911 jurisdiction. If you want reassurance, carry a personal security device and keep it in your hand (it does you no good if it's sitting in the bottom of your backpack!).
- Make eye contact to show you're paying attention. This makes the predator nervous and it's more likely you could identify him in a line-up. Don't stare him down, though, just look him over, so he knows you see him.
- Party responsibly. It's okay to have fun, but stop before you become impaired and unable to make sound decisions or defend yourself from an attack.
- Have a wingman who keeps an eye on you at parties to ensure you don't end up in trouble. Have them watch your drink for you when you dance or use the restroom to be

certain it isn't spiked with a date rape drug. If your wingman sees you leaving with someone, especially someone you or she doesn't know well, have her find you. Agree in advance to leave the party together.

- Walk in well-lit or populated areas. If you must walk alone, especially if at night in a deserted area, have self-defense protection handy.

- Walk or hang out with other people. Predators don't like to attack groups because they're more likely to meet resistance or be ganged up on.

- Keep your doors and windows locked in your dorm and car, and have automated exterior lights around your apartment door if you live off campus.

- Use a monitored alarm system. Homes and apartments that are monitored are three times *less* likely to be broken into.

- Get self-defense training that prepares you to fight off an attacker.

- Use personal security products or weapons to help defend yourself.

- If you live off campus, have a dog or make it obvious that you don't live alone. Leave a dog dish or a pair of men's work boots on your doorstep, even if you live alone.

- Set firm boundaries. Telling someone you don't know or who makes you uncomfortable to back off or leave you alone shows you're in charge and willing to defend yourself. Also, telling someone you DO know to stop if he makes inappropriate comments or jokes sends the message that you won't tolerate bad behavior.

CJ Scarlet

- Don't flash your money. Robbers lurk near ATMs for a reason, so if you must go to one, take someone with you or go during a busier time of the day when the bank is open.
- Let one or more people know where you're going, and when you expect to arrive or return when you go out. If you don't show up when you were expected to, you've left a trail for police to follow.
- Have your car keys (which can be used as a weapon to slash at the predator) or other security device in hand, and check the backseat of your car before getting in. Lock the doors as soon as you get in.
- Avoid getting into your car if a stranger is standing nearby or if you don't like the looks of the situation.
- Resist the perpetrator's commands by running away or fighting back (if you can do so). This is especially important if the predator tries to move you to another location (e.g., an alley or a car).
- Yell and run toward a public place if a predator confronts you.
- Report the predator to the police. (They really, really hate that!)

COMING UP NEXT...

In the next chapter, I'll share how to "fail" the predator interview and recognize when you're being groomed so you can thwart their plans. I'll cover the different kinds of predator interview techniques, how to conduct an interview of your own, and tips for recognizing and responding to danger. Finally, I'll provide great ways to decrease your chances of being targeted and, very importantly, I give you full permission to lie!

CHAPTER 7

How to "Fail" the Predator Interview

Kevin was a seasoned predator and knew exactly how to groom his victims. He selected confident but gentle women because he liked the challenge of beating them at a game in which only he knew the rules. This time he chose Trina, a manager with a large consulting firm. He could tell by her ready smile and quick intelligence that she trusted people, yet would make a worthy target.

He began with compliments about Trina's work, and when he could see she was flattered, he began commenting on her attractive appearance. Trina was a bit shy and smiled politely, which he liked. Over a period of several months, he tested Trina to see how she responded to his overtures, pushing a bit further every time.

One night in the hotel bar after a long day at a conference, Kevin bought Trina a drink. But it was no ordinary cocktail; it contained a powerful hallucinogen that almost immediately knocked her off her feet. Kevin told their co-workers Trina had imbibed too much and he was going to help her to her room. In actuality, he took her to his room and raped her.

Trina remembered flashes of the incident, but he assured her nothing had happened. At the same time, Kevin began spreading rumors about Trina— that she had a wild side, that she drank too much, that she was unpredictable and a bit crazy. Trina's friends were confused; they thought they knew her well, but as the rumors grew, doubt began to creep in. In addition to stealing Trina's innocence and dignity, Kevin worked to completely undermine her credibility as a witness if she ever told anyone.

In the end, Kevin raped and performed sex acts on Trina—all while she was drugged—over a period of six months. Trina only learned the truth when sex tapes of the violations surfaced. She didn't want to believe it was true and couldn't look at the videos. Horrified and in denial, Trina refused to press charges. She's certain Kevin had done it before and continued to do it again to other women.

Trina captures it perfectly, "Fundamentally it comes down to this: Rape is a holistic annihilation of one's self, replaced with the myth of someone who is slutty and untrustworthy and lacking in judgment. They (predators) take everything from you. That's what rape is about and why it's so hard to heal from it."

The Predator Has a Plan

WHETHER THEY'RE OPPORTUNISTIC criminals or sociopaths, predators usually have a plan in mind for how they're going to victimize you. Your goal is to thwart the predator in as many ways as possible so he'll decide you're a bad target and leave you alone. It's called *"failing the predator interview."*

According to Chuck and Kate O'Neill in *Psychological Self-Defense*, there are five stages predators go through in their minds when they're deciding whether to choose you as their victim.

The five stages are:

- **Observation**. Predators are on the look-out for someone vulnerable who they believe will be a "good" victim, meaning one who's unlikely to cause trouble. They may watch you for a period of time before making their move. But if you're equally observant of your environment and the people in it, you're more likely to spot potential danger and avoid it. For example, if you find yourself in a place that doesn't feel safe, say, a deserted parking lot, ask someone to escort you to your car. Security or campus police will be happy to walk with you if you feel unsafe.

- **Testing.** This is the part where the predator "interviews" you to determine whether you'll make a good target. The predator may gauge your posture, your willingness to look him straight in the eye, or your level of discomfort and fear in his presence. He might ask questions to find out if you're expecting someone to join you, or he may violate your space or make an inappropriate comment to see whether you'll be compliant or set personal boundaries.

- **Selection.** This is when the predator makes his decision about whether to assault you or leave you alone, based on the information he's gathered. Your behavior and reactions up to this point will sway his decision, for good or ill.

- **Isolation.** Predators will usually try to approach or move you to an isolated location to avoid discovery. This is when you, the potential victim, need to stand your ground and refuse to go anywhere with him, fleeing if you can. Even if he has a weapon, you're likely to be safer resisting him than complying with his demands to go with him.

- **Attack.** This is the moment when the predator tries to victimize you using physical force. And this is the moment when you must choose how to react to his attack. You have only seconds to decide whether to flee, fawn, fight, or comply, depending on what you think will result in the least harm to you.

How Predators Groom Their Victims

Grooming is one way predators manipulate their targets to gain their trust and then take advantage of them. They're pros at manipulating their victims into an emotionally vulnerable state and then victimizing them. They can quickly assess the strengths and weaknesses of their chosen victims, and decide which tactics will be the most effective for each person.

An example, used by criminal justice expert Gavin de Becker in his book *The Gift of Fear*, involves a man seated next to a young woman traveling alone on an airplane. Through seemingly casual conversation, the man is able to determine that she's naïve, that she's flattered by his attention, and that she's not meeting anyone at the airport. He offers to give her a ride to her destination, at which point he would likely have initiated an assault had not de Becker stepped in to warn the girl, who ended up declining the "free" ride. The key here is to be alert to probing questions, and to maintain your emotional and physical boundaries.

The mind is both a powerful and a fragile thing. It's important to remember that it's not uncommon to be influenced by others without a high level of awareness of what's happening. Sadly, some predators manipulate their targets so thoroughly that they (the victims) may come to believe the predator genuinely loves them. In return, they develop strong, loving feelings and come to depend on their abuser. This is especially common in relationships between intimate partners and cases such as child abuse involving a parent. If the victim is emotionally, physically, and financially dependent on the predator, it's easy to fall into his trap, and it becomes more difficult to resist or report him.

To be clear, I am NOT blaming the victim. There exists a power dynamic that may lead some people to become co-dependent because they believe it's the safest or most loving course of action. But it's never the person's fault if she's victimized; it's a choice the predator makes.

Predator Interview Techniques

Also in *Psychological Self-Defense,* Kate and Chuck O'Neill address general techniques predators use to determine your suitability for victimization:

THE STANDARD INTERVIEW

The standard interview may appear as an innocent question by a predator who may ask you for directions, for change, or to use your cell phone, all in an attempt to distract you. They're watching to see how you respond, whether you're engaged or disoriented by their questions, and whether you allow them to get close to you. To thwart him, be aware of who's around you and stay alert when someone approaches you. Keep him at least five feet away from you; if he tries to get closer, firmly tell him to back off. A simple, "Excuse me, but you're standing too close and it's making me uncomfortable," will do.

THE FAST AND FURIOUS INTERVIEW

This occurs when a predator attacks you from out of nowhere, the idea being that you'll be too shocked and disoriented to fight back. This type of interview happens fast, with little to no warning or talking. But there's still a type of interview process involved as the predator observes your behavior to determine whether you'll make a good target. He may be judging your body language, clothing, or even your shoes (to see if you can run in them). The best way to avoid this kind of attack is to appear clear and confident at all times. The more aware you are, the less likely you are to be targeted.

The Temperature-Rising Interview

This interview begins normally, but escalates into an attack. An example would be a campus rape, in which a young woman is talking with another student at a frat party. The conversation may proceed normally, but once they go to an isolated location to make out, the man may suddenly attack her. Obviously, you don't go to isolated locations with people you don't know well and completely trust.

The Extended Interview

This interview takes place over a longer period of time and you may become friends or even dating partners with this predator. The point of the extended interview is to understand your needs, hopes and dreams (to play to them), assess your strengths and weaknesses, and gain your trust—all to enable the predator to manipulate and deceive you.

Trina's situation is an example of this. This kind of predator may try to manipulate you or violate your physical and emotional boundaries. If this relationship reaches a point where you're not comfortable, the good news is you usually have time to end it before it goes any further.

If the predator persists in trying to see you, your best bet is not to engage with him, meaning you don't take his calls and you most certainly don't meet with him, no matter how insistent he becomes. In some situations, you may need to contact the police to file a stalking or harassment report and/or get an order of protection against him. Be prepared to protect yourself physically if he confronts you.

Conduct Your Own Interview!

You can turn the tables on a potential predator by doing your own "interview." Pay attention to the questions he asks and ask some of your own, such as "Why are you asking me that?" This will let the predator know you have strong boundaries. Don't forget that you can always lie to him to thwart his plans. You can say you're expecting your boyfriend (imaginary or otherwise) any second or that you're on your way to a gun range to test fire your gun.

If you're paying close attention to what he's saying and doing, he might reveal clues that will tip you off to his motives and, therefore, his potential for danger. Think about your surroundings and level of comfort with him. If you find yourself in a situation with someone you don't know or trust, assess and take notice of his behavior.

Remember to briefly make eye contact, keep your head up, and stay confident. Think of a situation or story you can tell as a way to test the situation. The story can be simple and easily remembered under pressure—that your father, boyfriend, or brother is meeting you in a few minutes, for example. If the predator is looking for clues of vulnerability on your part, then you must look for behavioral clues of aggressive or overly interested behavior on his. You can test him on where, when, and why he's asking you such things. The intent here isn't to escalate the situation, but to show confidence and thwart his attempts to groom you.

Predators are always assessing others to find potential victims. The stronger and more confident you appear, the less appealing you look to them. Awareness equals greater security!

Outwitting Predators

It's common sense; if you choose to engage in high-risk behavior, you're a more attractive target for predators. High-risk behavior consists of anything you do that compromises your safety, whether it's going for a walk on the beach with the cute guy you just met at a party or drinking so much that you aren't in control anymore.

I'm going to take a hit on this from people who say the responsibility shouldn't be on women and girls to alter their behavior to avoid victimization. I completely agree; however, this is the real world we live in and until men no longer treat women as objects, toys, or victims, we need to be practical. Please, please don't put yourself in harm's way because you're too embarrassed to ask for someone to walk you to your car after work, or too proud to admit that you're too drunk to function.

Below are just a few ways you can decrease your chances of being targeted by predators:

AWARENESS AND AUTHORITY

- If you're a student, become familiar with your campus. Know where the most dangerous spots are, and the safest routes to and from classes.
- If you use headphones when you run or walk around, use only one earbud so you can hear what's going on around you.
- Let someone know where you're going and when you expect to be back. If you can, download a mobile app that shares your location with police, or friends and family.
- Get familiar with your campus transportation system—most colleges have transportation to make sure their students get home safely at the end of a late night.
- Take one or more self-defense classes so you'll know what to do if attacked.
- Program your phone for 911 or campus security so it's a favorite or on speed dial. They should be informed of every potentially unsafe situation.

PARTYING AND DRINKING

- Perpetrators who drink prior to an assault are more likely to believe that alcohol increases their sex drive, and are also more likely to think that if a woman is drinking, it's a signal that she's interested in sex.[xli]

- Drinking or taking drugs is NOT an invitation to be raped. However, women are more vulnerable to rape if they've been drinking or doing drugs. Women are judged much more harshly than men if they're assaulted while impaired. And, as unfair as it is, men often use the excuse that they were too impaired to know what they were doing if accused of assaulting someone. Being in an assault situation where alcohol was present creates a whole new level of ambiguity about what happened. It amplifies the importance of being clear about intent.

- Don't be foolish—avoid drinking too much and never walk alone at night. Yes, you should be able to safely do whatever you want, but you need to be smart.

- Know what you have on you that can be used for self-defense, such as your keys, purse (when swung at a predator's head), mace, umbrella, etc. Of course, your best defensive tools are on your body—head (for head-butting), mouth (for yelling at the top of your lungs), teeth (for biting everything within reach), elbows and butt of the hand (for striking), fingers (for clawing, scratching, and pinching skin anywhere on the body), and knees and feet (for kicking).

- Plan how you're going to get home before you go out.

- Have a wingman whose job it is to keep an eye on how much you drink, who you hang out with, and who you leave with. Do the same for her/him.

- If you're on a date, decide ahead of time the level of sexual intimacy you're comfortable with and communicate that clearly with your date before you both start drinking. (Here's *a tip from Aunt CJ: When I was a young adult, a friend taught me that if I didn't want to have sex with my date that night, I shouldn't shave my legs beforehand. There was no way I was going to take my clothes off looking like a Yeti! That one piece of advice never failed to work.)*

- If it's possible there will be sexual activity, carry your own protection and don't rely on your partner to have a condom. If you have protection in your purse and you're later assaulted, the fact that protection wasn't used could help show that the incident was actually rape and not consensual.

- Remember that you ALWAYS have the right to stop sexual intimacy, even if you've had sex with that person before or may have consensual sex with them again in the future. But, please, be clear about your intentions so there's no confusion; guys can't read your mind. If you mean no, say it with conviction. If you want to engage in consensual sex, tell him so with a clear yes.

- Stay with a group of people you know and trust when you're at parties, and go home with the group you came with.

- If at a bar, watch the bartender make your drink. Never leave your drink unattended and don't accept cocktails from someone you don't know.

- Know your alcohol limits and stick to them. It's fun to get tipsy; it's less so to be so bombed that you can't fight back if you need to.

- Guys (and gals), if you see a woman being harassed, please intervene. You should also put a stop to any plan to intentionally get a woman intoxicated by drugs or alcohol to victimize her.

DRIVING AND LOGISTICS

- Bring cash with you so you can get out of a risky situation without having to find someone to borrow money from; this also enables you to avoid being at an ATM by yourself in a sketchy area.
- Taking a taxi or Uber ride will cost money, but it may save you from an attack.
- Don't give your personal details (phone number, address, etc.) to strangers. If you're interested in seeing them again, get their information so you can call them later. If they pressure you for your number, stand your ground and refuse, or give them a fake number.
- Keep your dorm or apartment doors locked, and don't share your keys with anyone or open the door to someone you don't know.
- If you find yourself in a dangerous situation, yell, run toward help, fight if you have to, and make a report (you just might save someone else from being victimized by doing so).
- If you receive inappropriate or threatening phone calls, text messages, or emails, tell someone and, if needed, report it to the police.
- Before you go out, ensure you have a full gas tank and a fully charged cell phone programmed to call 911 or campus police.
- Park your car under a street light or in an area with other people. Never walk to your car alone in a deserted area at night. If no one is leaving at the same time you are, ask a couple of friends to walk you to your car. Or call Security for an escort.

RECOGNIZING AND RESPONDING TO DANGER

- If someone is being too pushy or making you uncomfortable, tell them firmly to back off! Ask for help if you need it to shake off a guy who's being too persistent or who makes you uncomfortable.
- If you think you're being followed, don't ignore him. Stop, turn to face him, and with your hands up in a stop gesture, look him in the eye and say loudly and aggressively, "Are you following me?" or "Can I help you?" Do this and the person will likely back away and claim they weren't following you. They might also discount you as a suitable victim if they were planning an attack. Make sure your voice is loud and strong. Attackers don't want noisy, strong, aggressive, troublesome victims; they want victims who will be frightened and submissive.
- Trust your intuition and do whatever you must to get out of a situation that doesn't feel right to you.
- Set boundaries for yourself and stand in your power if someone crosses them. Don't be embarrassed or feel bad for sticking up for yourself. Fifteen seconds of embarrassment is worth it to avoid a lifetime of post-traumatic stress!
- If you decide to fight your attacker, remember that your body is a fearsome weapon that's at your disposal at all times.
- Make yourself a "bad victim." By yelling and fighting back (if you decide to do so), the attacker will realize you're not an easy target and will often leave.
- Confident body language can keep an attack from happening at all.

- Keep a personal security weapon and your cell phone by your bedside.
- You are worth fighting for! Don't apologize for standing up for yourself.

Some women have told me, with great concern, that if they avoid a predator, some other poor woman will become his victim. You can't think that way! Rather, think that you are making him even more wary of approaching another woman.

It's Okay to Lie

If you find yourself in an uncomfortable situation, like being pressured to have sex, you can use the following excuses to remove yourself from the situation:

- I have to work tomorrow.
- I wish I could, but I have to write a paper tonight.
- I have an exam tomorrow I need to study for.
- No thanks (for the drink); I'm the designated driver.
- No thanks; I've reached my limit.
- Sorry, I have a game tomorrow and want to be at my best, so I don't want to be out late.
- I have plans already.
- I wish I could (have a drink), but I'm on medication.
- My parents/roommate would kill me.
- I don't feel comfortable with that.
- No. I'm not ready to take that step yet.

- Sorry, I'm on my period.
- No.
- Stop!
- Help!
- Get away!
- I'm going to call the police if you don't stop (and then DO IT if they don't stop).

Coming Up Next...

It's go time! In Chapter 8, I'll tell you how to respond if you're confronted by a predator, including how to talk yourself out of the situation, and how to react if talking isn't working. I'll also touch on what to do if the predator wants to take you to a secondary location to further victimize you.

How to Respond If You're Confronted by a Predator

Seven-year-old Kimberly was grabbed by a man at a store in Atlanta when her mother's back was turned. The man tried to run off with Kimberly firmly in his grasp, but the 2nd grader put up a fight. She kicked and screamed until the perpetrator, who had recently been released from prison where he had served time on a murder charge, let her go and fled. He was later caught.

It's go time!

THE MOMENT YOU'VE been dreading and preparing for—confrontation with a predator—is at hand. Remember, YOU have a lot of power in this situation. You are NOT defenseless and you DON'T need to wait to be rescued.

Your choices in this moment will be a factor in what happens next. Take this opportunity to be tenacious and seek ways to remove yourself from the situation if you can. No matter how things play out, don't give up hope. The chance to thwart the predator could present itself at any moment.

Try to determine what the predator really wants. If it's your phone or purse, toss them away from you and run. If it's your body they're after and you can't run away, decide whether it's in your best interest to fight, fawn, or comply.

Talking Your Way Out of the Situation

If possible, attempt to unbalance the power the attacker is fighting to gain. As much as you can, maintain steady eye contact and talk to him in a calm, reasonable voice. The calmer you are, the more confident and powerful you appear. This will make the predator uncomfortable. You can try to relate to him by asking his name and telling him yours. Share that you have a husband or children (even if you don't) to make him see you as a human being and not just a nameless, faceless target.

Show you respect him by rephrasing and playing back what he says to you. For example, if he says, "Give me your purse," you might say, "You want my purse? Here you go" (throwing it away from you and running in the other direction). If he tells you to get in his car, you might say, "You want me to get in your car? That's not something I'm going to do."

Make random statements to throw the predator off his game, such as, "My ride is here," or, "Do you know what time it is?" You can also warn him that if he takes one more step, you'll yell for help—then actually begin yelling for help so he'll know you're serious.

If you have to, pee, poop, or throw up to make yourself a less attractive target. You could even pretend to have a seizure or heart attack, which some people have successfully done. These things will frighten or confuse the assailant, and might lead him to flee or offer you precious seconds to run away.

De-escalate the situation by framing things in the predator's best interest. It can help to remind him of the consequences of his actions: "Look, it isn't worth spending the rest of your life paying for this. You go your way and I'll go mine."

Tell bald-faced lies to scare the predator: "My boyfriend is on his way" or, "I used an app to call the police and they're on their way now." Or, better yet, call 911 on your cell phone and start describing what the predator looks like. If he knows the police are coming and that he can be identified, he'll likely run. (If you don't get an answer from 911 immediately, start talking anyway; the perpetrator won't know you're talking to hold music.)

If the predator tries to get you to submit by threatening another person at the scene or a beloved pet, run anyway. If you don't run and instead allow him to control you, then both you and the other victim(s) are lost. As difficult as it might be to leave someone behind, the most important thing you can do is summon help. Then the perpetrator knows the police will soon arrive and he'll be more likely to release the other person and flee.

When Talking Isn't Working
If these ideas don't work and the predator begins to physically attack you, begin yelling as loudly as you can (yelling is more powerful

than screaming, and it will help you breathe and make you sound more powerful). Loudly yelling "NO!" prepares your mind to defend your body, it can summon attention and help, and it will let the predator know you won't be an easy target.

Next, start breathing deeply from your belly and chest to summon your fury and innate self-protective behavior. Visualize your whole body as bright red with flames shooting out of your skin. Be outraged that this person is trying to hurt you and use that anger as rocket fuel to power your actions.

You're summoning your inner Taz. You're ready to respond to whatever happens next. If you can't flee and you must fight, do so with every ounce of ferocity in your being. You have my personal permission to defend yourself by fighting as dirty as you possibly can to survive the attack. As a whirlwind of fists and feet, teeth and elbows, you're a predator's worst nightmare!

Now MOVE!!! Begin fighting like that Tasmanian Devil for all you're worth!

YOUR BODY'S BADASS ARSENAL

Below I remind you of the ways you can use your powerful bodily weapons to defend yourself. *(I show you each of these moves on my video blog at* www.cjscarlet.com.) Please don't skip these descriptions, because I go into greater detail here than I did in Chapter 2.

Eyes. *Your Eyes:* Earlier I told you that when you spot someone coming toward you on the street, briefly make eye contact and quickly size him up. But if you're under attack, you want to maintain eye contact with your assailant as much as you can, to intimidate him and enable you to follow his eyes to predict his next move.

His Eyes: If you're in a furious fight for your life with the predator, go for his eyes with your fingers. Plant your thumbs into his eye sockets, with your fingers on either side of his face, and press as hard as you can. Keep pressing until you feel a popping sensation (meaning you've burst his eyeballs. *(Yes, I know, it's gross and icky and violent, but it may save your life. Would you rather poke his eyes out, or have him rape or kill you?)* If it's simply not in you to push all the way into his eye sockets, press hard enough to blind him so you can run away.

Posture. If you're unable to flee and have to fight, don't be afraid to fight from the ground. If the predator is much stronger, outweighs you, or has a longer reach, it may be to your advantage to do so. From the ground, you can lie on your back and use your feet to push and kick the perpetrator away from you. You can also prop yourself up on one elbow and lie on your side with one foot up and ready to kick furiously at him every time he gets within reach. He'll have a hard time getting close enough to pin you down without getting kicked in the face, gut, knees, or groin. If he tries to come at you from the other side, simply flip onto the other elbow and leg so you're always facing toward him.

Voice. Remember that your voice is one of the most powerful tools in your self-defense arsenal. You can use it softly to warn the perpetrator to back off, calmly to talk him into leaving you alone, or loudly to freak him out. Many women have talked themselves out of scary situations by being clever ("My boyfriend will be here any minute."), by being friendly ("Cool shoes!") or by changing the subject ("Do you know where the mall is?"). While you're fighting, screech, howl, and yell as loudly as you can to both bring attention to the situation and to scare him into running away.

Head. Whether you're being held from the front or behind, you can swing your head forward or backward into the predator's face or head. Your upper forehead is one of the hardest bones on your body, so don't be afraid to slam it into his nose or chin to snap his head back and give you a chance to get away.

Of course, you're also using your head, as in your mind, to constantly think of ways to outwit the predator. No matter how bleak things look, an opportunity to get away from him could present itself at any moment and you want to be ready. Use that badass brain of yours and win the day!

Teeth. Chomp down on any body part that comes close to your face. It doesn't matter where you bite him, it's going to hurt so bad he'll howl with pain. With luck, the attacker will stop whatever he's currently doing, giving you precious distance and time to get into a better fighting position or flee, if you can.

Elbow. The outside of your lower arm close to the elbow is incredibly strong and effective as a weapon. You can use that area to rapidly strike the predator's face and chest, even his groin and knees if you're below him. Because the elbow is so strong, it will inflict damage to the predator without hurting you much.

Palm. Use the butt of your open palm to hit upward onto predator's chin or nose, which will snap his head back and make his eyes water so you can run away. As with the elbow, your palm can deliver a serious blow without hurting you much, if at all. Even just pushing his chin or nose up with the butt of your hand will force his head back away from you, and possibly enable you to maneuver to a better fighting position.

You can also cup your hand and slap the predator's head or face. I'm not talking little swats with your hand, which are largely ineffective; I'm talking about delivering a blow so hard it will make his ears ring for a week.

Fist. Unless you've trained to do so, punching someone with your fist can be awkward and ineffective. You'd do better using your closed fist and forearm to pound on the attacker like a hammer. (Remember: Keep your thumbs on the outside of your fists or you could break your fingers!)

Fingers. Pinching and twisting the predator's skin is *incredibly* painful for him. Grab the skin and twist as hard as you can and don't let go until he backs off. The best spots to pinch are where the skin is thinnest, like the thighs and upper arms. But if you pinch and twist hard enough, it'll hurt no matter where you do it. You can also use your fingers to gouge and scratch the attacker's eyes and skin, dragging away bits of his DNA that may become critical later to proving the case against him.

Knees. Use your knee to kick the perpetrator in the groin when you're in close range. Know that if you go straight for the groin, the perp is going to see it coming and shift his body to avoid it. So, you want to distract him by acting like you're going to hit him in the face. Then, when he puts up his hands to block your strike, that's the time to kick him in the groin just as hard as you possibly can.

And, when he doubles over with pain, you can grab the back of his head and smash his face into your knee.

I know, this is brutal stuff, but your badass bod and life are at stake here and you need to fight as ferociously as you can.

Feet. Your feet, especially your heels, can be dangerous when you swipe, stomp, and kick any of the predator's body parts as violently as you can manage.

If you summon your inner Taz and become a whirlwind of fists and fangs and feet, he won't know what hit him and you increase your chances of getting away.

It's important to remember that while you're going absolutely bonkers on the predator's ass, he's probably not going to just stand there and take it. He's likely going to go after you with equal or greater fury. Just keep fighting for all you're worth. Fight through the pain until you can escape.

Don't stop until:

- The predator stops his attack.
- The predator flees the scene.
- You've disabled the predator enough that he can't follow you if you run away.
- Help arrives and you're safe from the predator.

Secondary Crime Scenes

Some predators will want to take you to a more isolated, secondary location where they can do what they want with you out of sight of other people. This is better for him and far worse for you. Your chances of being seriously injured or killed increase in this scenario. Your chances of fleeing also go down. No matter how much you're threatened, with or without a weapon, it's always a bad idea to comply with this request.

According to Sam Harris in his article, *The Truth About Violence: 3 Principles of Self-Defense*, "If you find yourself in a situation where a predator is trying to control you, the time for listening to instructions and attempting to remain calm has passed. It will get no easier to resist and escape after these first moments."

Harris adds that the details—the presence of weapons, or the size and number of attackers—is irrelevant. He continues, "However bad the situation looks, it will only get worse [if you give in]. To hesitate is to put yourself at the mercy of a sociopath. You have no alternative but to explode into action, whatever the risk. Recognizing when this line has been crossed, and committing to escape at any cost is more important than mastering physical techniques."

Remember, you have more power than you think and can exercise it to escape dangerous situations. So let loose your inner Taz!

COMING UP NEXT...

Chapter 9 is geared toward girls and young women, who are the most vulnerable and, therefore, most often targeted by predators. The statistics I share will make your hair stand on end!

Violence Against Girls and Young Women

Erin was 14 the first time she had sex. She was so afraid—of disappointing her boyfriend Brian, of disobeying her parents, of the act itself—but she was more afraid that if she didn't give in, he would break up with her and find someone else.

Erin was crazy about Brian and was so fearful of losing him that she overlooked the times when he went into rages and sometimes slapped her, or when he forced her to do things sexually that she was uncomfortable with. She just knew that if she loved him enough, he would change. It was only when her parents spotted bruises around her neck that they found out what was going on and forced her to end the relationship.

Younger Women Are at Highest Risk

IN THIS EXAMPLE of partner violence, Erin had reason to fear breaking up with Brian. Nearly 20 percent of teenage girls reported that their boyfriends threatened to harm them or themselves if they broke up.

I'm telling you this not to scare you into staying in the relationship, but to scare you into leaving at the very first sign that something is off. Women and girls often choose bad boys or guys with problems, thinking they can change them and make them into better people. They think that if they're nice enough, the man or boy will start being nice to them. But the truth is, you can't love someone into not hurting you if they're a violent person.

It happens, too, that you might not feel worthy of being treated well and believe you're deserving of abusive behavior. Intimate relationships can be incredibly difficult, but there is NEVER any excuse for physical abuse of any kind.

Shockingly, two older surveys of sixth through ninth grade students conducted by the Rhode Island Rape Crisis Center found that many young people believe forced sex is acceptable under some circumstances. The survey of boys and girls, ages 11 to 14, found that half thought forced sex was acceptable if the boy "spent a lot of money" on the girl; 65 percent of boys and 47 percent of girls said it was acceptable for a boy to rape a girl if they had been dating for more than six months; and 87 percent of boys and 79 percent of girls said sexual assault was acceptable if the man and woman were married.[xlii]

Although teenage girls are the most likely to be victimized, they're the least likely to report it when they're assaulted. Having just been given permission to date, they may be reluctant to tell their parents when their date or boyfriend is abusive because they fear they won't be allowed to date anymore. In truth, telling your parents when you're in danger shows that you're mature enough and have solid enough judgment to make good dating choices.

If you're a parent, you should ask lots of questions to gauge the health and safety of your child's new relationships. If you suspect your child is in an abusive relationship or may have been sexually assaulted, don't hesitate to talk with her to discover the truth. Chances are, she's dying to talk to someone she can trust, but is afraid of getting into trouble herself.

The College Experience

High school students who plan to continue on to college are filled with hopes and dreams of the new life they'll live at university. Rosy pictures of success, fun, and social exploration dance in their heads. It's a time of extreme growth, and for the first time, young men and women are interacting without parental guidance and are being exposed to new situations when their hormones are still raging.

Here are some shocking statistics about college violence. Some may be hard to believe, but they're real, and preparing for this reality is important. If you're a parent preparing your daughter or son for college, please share these statistics and discuss the long-term effects of their behavior.

STATS TO MAKE YOU SIT UP AND PAY ATTENTION

- 80 percent of college students will drink alcohol while in college; half will engage in binge drinking.[xliii]
- Nearly 3.5 million students between the ages of 18 and 24 drove under the influence of alcohol in 2016.[xliv]
- In 81 percent of alcohol-related sexual assaults, both the victim and perpetrator had consumed alcohol.[xlv]
- Nearly 100,000 students between 18 and 24 become victims of alcohol-related sexual assault or date rape each year.[xlvi] 90 percent were committed by someone the victim knew.[xlvii]
- An estimated 400,000 college students have unprotected sex and more than 100,000 students report being too intoxicated to know if they consented to having sex.[xlviii]
- A survey of students from 32 colleges found that 54 percent of women had experienced some form of sexual assault. Only 5 percent of rape survivors reported the incident to the police. 42 percent told no one about the assault.[xlix]
- A staggering 84 percent of young women experience a sexually coercive event in their first two years in college.[l]
- Among undergraduate students, 23.1 percent of female and 5.4 percent of male students experienced rape or sexual assault through physical force, violence, or incapacitation.[li]
- Among graduate and professional students, 8.8 percent of females and 2.2 percent of males experienced rape or sexual assault through physical force, violence, or incapacitation.[lii]

- 7 percent of college males admitted to committing rape or attempted rape; 63 percent of them admitted to multiple offenses, for an average of six rapes each.[liii]
- College students who've been assaulted experience high rates of post-traumatic stress disorder, depression, and drug or alcohol abuse, which can hamper their ability to succeed in school.[liv]
- Depression and anxiety are linked to higher college dropout rates.[lv]

If the problem is so huge, why are so few incidents reported? Well, aside from feelings of shame and humiliation, young people may fear getting into trouble because they engaged in under-age drinking or were under the influence of drugs at the time. In fact, 75 percent of the men and 55 percent of the women involved in acquaintance rapes were drinking or taking drugs before the attack happened.[lvi] They may also blame themselves for their choices and fear they won't be believed if they report, knowing it's a "he said, she said" situation.

Party Rape

"Party rape" occurs at on- or off-campus fraternities or housing, and involves males encouraging young women to drink heavily or targeting intoxicated women. A 2007 study found that 58 percent of rapes involving incapacitated victims and 28 percent of forced rapes took place at parties.[lvii]

Many fraternities in the Greek system have come under fire for using parties where drugs and alcohol are freely available to sexually exploit young women. The objectification of women is often encouraged in that environment, which teaches young men to trivialize and even celebrate the rape of women.

Perpetrators who drink prior to an assault are more likely to believe that alcohol increases their sex drive – and are also more likely to think that a woman's drinking itself signals that she's interested in sex.[lviii] Drinking or taking drugs is NOT an invitation to be raped. However, women are more vulnerable to rape if they've been drinking or doing drugs.

Speaking of drugs, it's not only the ones you voluntarily ingest that you need to worry about. Predators, particularly while in college, may use Rohypnol ('roofies') or dozens of other date rape drugs which can't be seen, smelled, or tasted to incapacitate their victims. Common side effects include drowsiness, amnesia, impaired judgment, and a loss of coordination that can last for hours afterward. These drugs are also difficult to detect through blood tests after they've worn off.

Being in an assault situation where alcohol was present creates a whole new level of ambiguity about what happened, and it amplifies the importance of being clear about intent.

Coming Up Next...

In Chapter 10, I discuss the growing problem of human trafficking and how victims are groomed to become sex slaves. I also provide a wealth of tips on how to protect yourself when traveling to other countries.

CHAPTER 10

Modern Day Slavery

When I was 18, I was befriended by a woman who choreographed the dance routines of a play I performed in. Charlotte, an artist, was in her early 30s and when she asked me to model for her and her mother, I was flattered and agreed.

As I sat in various stages of undress before them, we chatted amiably about our hopes and dreams. I shared my burning desire to leave the small Arkansas town I felt trapped in and of my dreams of traveling the world, meeting fascinating people, and having exotic adventures.

Shortly after my 19th birthday, Charlotte called and asked if I was serious about leaving Arkansas. When I said yes, she told me she had good news and to come to her house right away. When I got to the rural home she shared with her parents, Charlotte sat me down on her bed and informed me that a wealthy man in Florida had seen one of her paintings of me and wanted me to be his mistress. My stomach began to clench and I could hear distant alarm bells ringing in my head as she continued.

Charlotte told me that with my new lover, I would—you guessed it—travel the world, meet fascinating people, and have exotic adventures. The man would also pay for me to go to college, and (here's the kicker), if I was a good mistress, the man would marry me and take care of me for the rest of my life.

I had no idea how to respond. By that time, the bells were clamoring in my head and my intuition was screaming at me to get the hell out of there. But before I could react, Charlotte's father walked into the room and she left. He proceeded to tell me that he would drive me to Florida and provide the "training" required for me to be a proper mistress. Then he attempted to sodomize me.

Gagging and terrified, I found the courage to leap from the bed and run outside to my car. I managed to lock the door just as he grabbed the handle. As I tore out of the driveway, gravel flying behind me, I could hear him yell, "Don't you DARE tell!"

For years I didn't tell a soul. It was a decade later before it occurred to me that there was no wealthy *man waiting for me. With dawning horror, I realized the more likely plan was to get me to Florida under the control of some pimp who would force me into using drugs and walking the streets as a prostitute.*

It was another decade before I heard the term "human trafficking," but I recognized it as soon as I heard it. I also realized, after sharing this experience with a high school friend, that Charlotte and her father had done this to other young women. Charlotte has since moved and her father died, but I wonder to this day how many girls were trafficked because I didn't tell.

It's More Common Than You Think

HUMAN TRAFFICKING IS one of the most prevalent criminal activities on the planet, outpaced only by the drug and arms trades. It's used to line the pockets of predators who are willing to coerce human beings into sexual slavery and exploitation, and the forced labor of children and adults.

The International Labour Organization estimates that human trafficking and forced labor is a $150 billion worldwide industry.[lix] Polaris, a U.S.-based source of information about trafficking and support for victims, states that 21 billion people are victims of trafficking globally today, and that there are hundreds of thousands of victims in the U.S. alone.[lx]

Young women and children are particularly vulnerable to sexual slavery and exploitation. 26 percent of victims are children; 55 percent are women and girls.[lxi] Predators may carefully groom victims (as in my case) and then use lies, threats of harm, and violence to coerce them into sexual slavery or labor. Some also use professed love (yes, love) for their victims to convince then that prostituting themselves will help the predator and victim financially.

How Predators Choose Their Trafficking Victims

There are several reasons predators choose particular victims, but there are also patterns they look for in their targets' behavior that provide clues you can use to avoid them. The most essential thing a predator must do to groom his victim is to establish her trust in him.

Predators look first for women and children who lack self-confidence; who need someone to listen to and understand them; to flatter them; to reassure them that they're special, attractive, smart, or cool. Predators work to learn their targets' likes and dislikes, habits and fears, and they pretend to share these feelings. They may buy them gifts and shower them with praise, all to convince their targets they're special and loved.[lxii]

They also cater to their victims' need for approval and recognition, to the point that their victims may become emotionally or psychologically dependent on them, which further increases the predators' ability to manipulate them. It's a vicious cycle that increases the chances that they'll be able to successfully exploit their targets.[lxiii] All this makes it easier for the predator to continue to use and manipulate his victim. And, with time, the victim may allow the abuse to continue because she's dependent on him for his financial support, or fears she will be harmed or killed if she leaves.[lxiv]

What You Need to Know About Sex Trafficking

WHO ARE THE VICTIMS?

Victims of human trafficking come from every race, social class, immigration status, and income level. Women and children are the most vulnerable; as are people who have little education, live in poverty, come from a marginalized population, are dependent on drugs, or grew up in an abusive home. Runaways, especially, are at tremendous risk of being trafficked.

According to the website DoSomething.org, the average age of children lured into the sex trade in the United States is 12 to 14 years old. Yes, you read that correctly. Many of them are runaway girls who were sexually abused as children. The website estimates that over 100,000 American children are forced into pornography or prostitution each year. More are shipped overseas and sold to the highest bidder as sex slaves.

WHO ARE THE TRAFFICKERS?

Sex traffickers also come from every walk of life. They're opportunistic criminals and professional groomers, always on the prowl for new victims; that's how they make their living. They have absolutely no compassion for their victims or compunction about forcing them into sexual slavery.

Traffickers hold up the promise of a better life for their victims, offering them money, gifts, attention, and affection. In reality, they exploit their victims, forcing them into prostitution, and often getting them addicted to drugs in order to make the victims dependent on them.

WAYS TO SPOT A TRAFFICKER

The old adage is true: if something looks too good to be true, it probably is. Again, you must pay heed to your gut and intuition in situations where you're approached by someone who promises a better life. Trust me, there's a catch. If you're not sure whether to trust a person who offers you a quick, easy way to make money or to leave your mundane existence behind, do your homework.

Conduct a background check on him/her and see what comes up. They may be using a false name, so an Internet search or background check may not provide much information. A good way to see if the offer passes the smell test is to talk about it with a trusted teacher/parent/friend. Because they're outside the situation, they'll be in a good position to see if the deal sounds suspicious.

You can also "interview" the person making the offer to see how he reacts to your questions. Is he evasive in his answers when you ask for more details about the opportunity? Does he tell you to just "trust" him without answering your questions? Does he try to minimize your concerns? Does he attempt to isolate you, or turn you against your friends and family? Is he possessive or verbally/emotionally/physically/sexually abusive in any way?

Run, do not walk away from this situation. I'm serious; end all contact and report that person to the police. Your report may stop him from luring any other unsuspecting person into sex slavery.

Avoiding Traffickers Outside Your Home Country

Below are some tips to follow to avoid being groomed or trafficked when traveling outside your home country:

- Before you leave or when you arrive in the new country, register with the local U.S. embassy. Know the address and telephone number of the embassy closest to where you're staying. Alert them of your travel plans and keep their contact information with you at all times.
- Leave breadcrumbs (information on your whereabouts) by registering your travel plans at: http://travel.state.gov/ and http://travel.gc.ca.
- When traveling abroad, sign up for the Smart Traveler Enrollment Program. Enter information about your trip so the U.S. Department of State can help you in an emergency.
- Before you travel, look at the local news online of the places you plan on visiting so you know what's going on and can know which areas to avoid.
- Carefully guard your passport, which can be worth a small fortune on the black market. Make sure you keep a copy of your passport information in a safe place where only you can find it. Do the same with your credit and ID cards.

- Don't post your travel plans on social media or discuss them in public places.
- Learn to speak enough of the local language to get around and get yourself help if you need it. You can also download Google Translator or other app on your phone so you can communicate with locals.
- Check online to see how far the airport is from your hotel so you don't get taken by the taxi driver.
- *NEVER* share a cab with a stranger.
- Don't trust strangers who volunteer to give you a tour of the town. Do an online search for a well-known tour company.
- Dress according to local customs. American women tend to dress more informally than many countries' cultures find acceptable. Standing out in a more conservative country can make you a target for violence.
- If you're traveling solo, check into your hotel as "Mr. and Mrs. X, so people think you have a partner with you.
- If you're going out for the day, leave a note in your hotel room explaining where you're headed.
- Beware of strangers. Sex traffickers often seem harmless and might be well-dressed, young, and good looking. Don't ever tell a stranger your full name, where you are going, or if you're staying alone.
- Avoid unsafe situations. Don't travel alone at night or on deserted side streets. If you think you're being followed, head toward a crowded place. Don't hesitate to alert police to your suspicions, and give them a description of the potential perpetrator.

- Volunteer with caution. When traveling abroad for volunteer opportunities, only pick reputable agencies that have strict protocols and thorough supervision. Before you sign up with an organization, do some research to make sure they're a legitimate charity organization. Be aware that there are organizations that try to exploit foreign citizens.
- Many traffickers are associated with bands of cybercriminals who use Internet personas to groom victims online and in person.
- Never, never, never meet someone you've chatted with online in person until you know for certain they're legitimate. There's no reason for any child to meet in person with someone they're corresponding with on the Internet unless the parents have vetted them. More than 90 percent of children who meet online predators in person end up being abused by them. 90 percent![lxv]
- If you're a woman with children and you're being stalked, you may not be the primary or only target of a sexual predator or trafficker. Your children may be at risk, so report the predator to the police as soon as you suspect you or your children are being targeted.
- Support responsible businesses. If you see a club or bar that employs extremely young-looking workers or seems to be engaged in questionable practices, don't give them your business. If you do witness or hear about suspicious behavior, make a report to the police and to the Polaris Project.[lxvi]
- Don't support trafficking. Don't give money to child beggars who may be the victims of trafficking. If you give money to

these children, you're helping the trafficking industry remain profitable. Instead, donate money to a local charity, school, or clinic.

COMING UP NEXT...

In Chapter 11, I cover exactly what to do if you've been the victim of a crime and, just as important, what NOT to do. I'll share how to get immediate help, questions you can expect to be asked by the police, and how to report the assault to your Title IX coordinator (if you're a student). I also address why it's so important to make a report, even if you don't choose to press charges against the assailant.

CHAPTER 11

If You've Been Victimized

IT HAPPENED. YOU'VE been the victim of a crime. I'm so sorry this happened to you. Know it wasn't your fault and that you did nothing to deserve it. The perpetrator deserves all the blame for choosing to commit the offense.

Now what? There are decisions to be made, and at a time when you may feel least able to make them. Your mind and body are numb, or you're completely freaked out. You may be faced with people who are peppering you with questions: "Are you okay?" "Do you need an ambulance?" "Do you want to report the crime?" Time seems to be whirring by and everything is foggy. Who do you tell? How do you handle the police, your attacker, your life?

The purpose of this chapter is to tell you what your options are and the consequences of the choices you make in the critical hours following your assault.

Mission Critical: Immediately After the Assault

The assault is over, and the perpetrator has either left the scene or you were able to get away from him. The first order of business is to find safety and help. If you're not safe at that location or you fear the predator will return, leave immediately and get to the house of a friend, to the police station, or to a populated location where you're surrounded by people who can help you.

If you still have your cell phone or access to someone else's phone, call 911 immediately. You may also want to call a friend or family member to be with you, but _don't make that call until you or someone you've connected with has talked with the 911 operator_ and asked them to dispatch someone to your location.

If you approach a group of people, it's important that you single out one person and tell them to call 911. Interestingly, people in groups tend to assume someone else will take responsibility for summoning help, which has led many victims to receive none! Point to just one person and tell them to make the call.

Pay close attention to your body. While you may have suffered trauma to your pelvic area, you may also have injuries to other parts of your body that need more immediate attention. If so, tell the operator you need medical assistance so they can call an ambulance. Some injuries, such as a concussion, or symptoms like internal pain may not appear until hours or days after the event, so it's important to be examined by a medical professional.

What NOT to Do After an Assault

Following an assault, your body and clothing may contain critical evidence that could help police catch the predator and take him off the street before he hurts someone else. It's imperative that you carefully maintain any physical evidence of the attack.

This means you must remain in or safeguard the clothing you were wearing during the attack, including your bra and underwear, and not try to clean them. It means you don't take a bath or shower right away. It means you don't eat or drink anything, or brush your teeth if you were orally sodomized (meaning he placed his penis or semen onto or into your mouth).

I know. You want to scour all evidence of that monster's presence from your body, but I caution you to *please* delay. Just don't do it; not yet. You may think in that moment that you'll never press charges, but you're under enormous strain, and after the adrenaline has worn off and you've had some time away from the attack, you may change your mind. The statutes of limitations for reporting an assault vary by state, and you need evidence if you choose to report your attack.

So, please:

- No showers.
- No consumption of food, drinks, or alcohol.
- No brushing your teeth.
- No manicures or heavy scrubbing of nails.
- No washing hair.
- No disposing of items on your person during the attack.
- No deleting any written or digital evidence of your whereabouts during the time of the attack.

Reporting the Assault to Police

A violent crime occurs in the U.S. every 10 seconds.[lxvii] One of every three women in the world will be beaten or abused during her lifetime; one in five will be raped.[lxviii] According to RAINN.org, the average rapist assaults six people before being caught. Yet only a fraction of victims ever reports their offenders.

If the problem is so huge, why are so few incidents reported? Well, aside from feelings of shame and humiliation, people may fear being blamed for the attack or getting into trouble because they engaged in illegal behavior around the time of the incident.

Because reports aren't made, fewer than 1 percent of rape cases result in convictions for the offenders.[lxix]

There are logical and solvable reasons for this:

- **A lack of corroborating evidence**. Most rape and domestic violence incidents are "he said, she said" cases, meaning it's one person's word against another's, with little or no corroborating evidence to back them up. The victim may fear being dragged through the mud, while the perpetrator is unlikely to face any meaningful consequences.
- **Victim mentality**. As mentioned above, the crime survivor may blame herself or feel embarrassed because of her actions surrounding the incident (e.g., she was drinking or on drugs), or she may question herself whether the assault really happened the way she remembers.
- **Victim blaming**. On top of having to deal with the psychological burden of the crime, survivors face enormous negative social judgment. They're told the assault was their fault because they were drunk or wore the mini skirt or went to the party.

- **Protecting the perpetrator**. Family, friends, coaches, or employers may circle the wagons around the perpetrator and villainize the survivor.
- **A broken system**. Universities, prosecutors, judges, or the police may be unsupportive, defensive, or even hostile, discouraging survivors from reporting. Additional pressure not to report may also come from loved ones, due to their own embarrassment, disbelief, or fear.

Survivors are more likely to press charges if they have the support of friends and family, actively resisted the attack, were assaulted by a stranger, were physically injured, or if a weapon was used. The common denominator here is that these incidents were clearly assaults, as opposed to incidents such as date rape that are more ambiguous.

Why Pressing Charges is So Important

Reporting your assault to police is NOT the same as pressing charges against your assailant. Whether or not you decide to press charges—and you don't have to decide that right way—it's critical that you report the crime to the police. They need to know a predator is on the loose because other people (or you!) could be in danger. They may also be looking for that very person and your account could give them just the information they need to catch him.

Pressing charges, on the other hand, is an intensely personal decision, one that takes a great deal of thought and courage, but there are several reasons to do so:

- **Convictions are a deterrent.** Prosecution of offenders is meant to act as a deterrent to others, to convince them the crime isn't worth the time. When predators aren't held accountable, other people may feel they, too, can get away with their crimes.
- **Predators WILL find new victims.** Rapist and child molesters, especially, are generally serial offenders. According to a study conducted by David Lisak and Paul M. Miller, rapists commit an average of 6.2 rapes before being caught.[lxx] If your perpetrator is apprehended, your testimony could take him off the streets and ensure he can't get access to more victims.
- **Your experience helps educate law enforcement.** If more people reported their assaults, law enforcement would have more information about the dynamics of sexual assault and how to prevent it.
- **You're able to claim your power.** Nothing is more empowering than standing up for yourself and protecting your boundaries. When you press charges against your attacker and testify against him, you're speaking your truth and taking your power back!
- **You encourage other survivors.** When you press charges and testify against the perpetrator, you're empowering other survivors to bring their offenders to justice too.

Whether you decide to report your assault and/or press charges against your assailant is up to you, but I hope you'll give the idea your greatest consideration. If you're not sure what to do, talking with a counselor at your local rape crisis center, campus Title IX office (if you're a student) or Women's Center can be very helpful.

What the Police Will Want to Know

While you're waiting for the police to arrive, try to recall details of the event so you can report them. Write down every detail that comes to mind or ask someone to write them down for you. You can capture them on a cell phone app or take an audio recording as they come to mind. Try to remember the sights, sounds, smells, and feelings you experienced during the attack.

Questions the police are likely to ask you:

- What events occurred leading up to the assault?
- Where did the assault happen? Were you taken from one location to another?
- When did the assault occur? Was it dark or light outside? Can you recall the exact time?
- Who did you talk to and could any of those conversations be relevant?
- Can you identify any distinguishing features of the predator?
- What color were his eyes, skin, hair?
- What were his approximate height and weight?
- Did he have any tattoos, scars, or moles?
- Was he wearing unusual jewelry, such as rings or a watch?
- What can you remember about the clothing he wore?

- Do you recall any threats or statements the perpetrator made, or keywords he used? Did he say anything strange (for example, calling you by someone else's name during the attack)?
- Did the predator use any weapons to threaten or harm you?
- What injuries did you receive?
- What injuries did the attacker receive?
- How did the incident end?
- Were any of your belongings disrupted or stolen?

Please understand that as hard as it was to experience the assault, the process of working with the police afterward can be difficult in its own way. You'll be faced with questions and procedures that your mind and body may not be prepared for because you're in a state of shock.

When the police arrive, they'll first check to see if you need medical attention. Next, they'll want to know any details you can provide about the assault and the perpetrator. It's okay if you can't remember every detail during the first interview. If they ask you a question and you don't know the answer, just tell them you can't remember right now.

It's also okay if you can't give a statement right away because you feel dissociated, numb, hysterical, or too fearful to recall events. The police are trained to ask questions in ways that might help you remember what happened. If you're unable to give a statement immediately after the assault, they can interview you later, when your memory has become more clear.

POLICE ARE ONLY HUMAN

While it's nice to think every police officer and investigator will listen compassionately to your story and ask questions that validate the serious nature of your experience, that's not always the case. "Second victimization" occurs when the responding officers don't take your report seriously. This may be due to their own personal bias, your relationship to the perpetrator, or because of your behavior prior to or during the attack.

If you were drinking, taking drugs, or were alone in a dangerous neighborhood at night, you might sense judgment or a lack of interest during questioning. If you feel confused or dissociated and your story is inconsistent, the police may decide you're lying and consider your claim as a false report.

Police officers are human and some cling to rape myths. If you feel the police aren't taking you seriously or are asking inappropriate questions, ask to speak to their superior officer. If they won't let you talk to anyone else, end the interview and call your local rape crisis center or the national sexual assault hotline for help. (See Appendix for a list of resources.)

The fact is, the Supreme Court of the United States ruled that police are not obligated by law to protect us. Heck, they don't even have to show up if they're called.[lxxi] Fortunately, they generally do show up and do take crimes seriously, but you may find it necessary to rely on other sources of help if they don't.

If you don't feel safe during this initial reporting phase, remember, this is normal; you were just violated and then asked to trust a complete stranger with the most intimate details of your being. Please try not to absorb further blame or shame from an authority figure after your assault. You're not to blame here and it doesn't diminish the severity of the crime or your character in any way. And know that most law enforcement and campus police officers take these crimes very seriously and are compassionate people.

Title IX: A Reporting Option for Students

(Note: as of the writing of this book, the status of Title IX was in question. If you're a student, check with your school's Administration Office to see whether they still have a Title IX coordinator for you to talk to.)

Title IX is a federal civil right that prohibits sex-based and other types of discrimination in education (K-12 schools, and colleges and universities). Most people think Title IX is just about sports, but it's also a prohibition against sex-based discrimination in education, including sexual harassment, gender-based discrimination, and sexual violence (including attempted or completed rape or sexual assault, sexual harassment, stalking, voyeurism, exhibitionism, verbal or physical sexuality-based threats or abuse, and intimate partner violence). The law protects any student from sex-based discrimination, regardless of their real or perceived sex, gender identity, and/or gender expression.

KnowYourIX.org states that, "If a school knows or reasonably should know about discrimination, harassment, or violence that is creating a "hostile environment" for any student, it must act to eliminate it, remedy the harm caused, and prevent its recurrence. Schools may not discourage survivors from continuing their education, such as telling them to 'take time off' or forcing them to quit a team, club, or class. You have the right to remain on campus and have every educational program and opportunity available to you."[lxxii]

Every school has a Title IX coordinator (hopefully) whose job is to follow established procedures for handling Title IX complaints. (To find your Title IX coordinator, look on your school's website or call the Administration Office.) Your school's Title IX office must investigate Title IX cases _even if they occur off campus._

What Happens After You File

If you file a Title IX complaint, your school's Title IX coordinator must promptly investigate the incident, even if you also report the incident to the local police, and should complete their investigation within the same semester it was reported. _(Note: Only report your assault to the Title IX Office AFTER you've reported it to your local and/or campus police. The police will do a more thorough investigation in an attempt to capture and convict the perpetrator, which the Title IX Office cannot do.)_

If, according to the school's investigation, the harassment or violence did occur, the perpetrator will be disciplined. Both you and the accused will be notified of the findings in writing, and both of you have the right to appeal the decision.

You're Protected from Retaliation and Contact with the Accused

Your school can't retaliate against you if you file a complaint and it must keep you safe from the retaliation of others. If your school or any person attempts to retaliate against you, you can make a formal Title IX complaint directly to the U.S. Department of Education's Office of Civil Rights.[lxxiii]

If needed, your school can issue a "no contact" order to keep the accused person from approaching or interacting with you in any way. Although this isn't the same as a court-issued restraining order (which you can also file for), your campus police should enforce the order if you notify them of a violation by the perpetrator.

Mediation and Formal Hearings

While schools can offer mediation for lesser crimes, when the case involves any type of sexual violence, mediation is prohibited and they must hold a formal hearing of the complaint. It's your choice to request a disciplinary hearing if you want the case to go through the formal process. The Title IX administrator is not supposed to allow the accused to question you during a hearing. If the school tries to allow that, seek the services of a nonprofit attorney or legal advocate to help you throughout the hearing, or file a Title IX complaint directly with the U.S. Department of Education.

Disciplining the Perpetrator

If it's determined the offense in question did occur and the accused is found guilty, disciplinary action may be taken against the perpe-trator, ranging from mandatory counseling to expulsion from the school. The reason it's important to also report your incident to the local police (whether or not it occurred on campus) is that they can bring criminal charges against the perpetrator that may result in stiffer penalties, including incarceration.

MAKING ACCOMMODATIONS

After the incident, you may want or need special accommodations to enable you to feel protected from the perpetrator and keep you safe. These may include, but aren't limited to, changes to your class schedule, tutoring, counseling, changes to your housing situation, and solutions for addressing your grades if you drop out of classes due to the incident or resulting trauma.

Accommodations can be put in place even before you make a formal complaint by talking to the Title IX coordinator. They also can continue after the entire process is over. You shouldn't be asked to pay for the cost of these accommodations. If your school fails to promptly take steps to eliminate the violence and prevent its recurrence, it may be required to reimburse expenses related to their lack of action, possibly including your tuition.

For a list of the types of accommodations you may be eligible to receive, visit http://knowyourix.org/violence-costs/. To ensure your rights are being protected and you receive all the accommodations you need, talk with your Title IX coordinator and/or Women's Center on campus. You can also contact your local rape crisis center for more help. (See Appendix for a list of resources.)

COMING UP NEXT...

In the next chapter, I'll focus on the reasons for getting a forensic rape exam if you've been sexually assaulted and the process involved. Not only might this exam capture evidence that may lead to an arrest and conviction in your case, it may also identify and protect you from pregnancy and sexually transmitted diseases. This chapter may be tough to read, but it's important for you to know the details before making that choice.

CHAPTER 12

Collecting the Evidence

The Forensic Rape Exam

THE INFORMATION IN this section is graphic. Knowledge is power, and the more you know about what your options are, the more confident and powerful you'll feel when making choices about your own care options.

If you've been sexually assaulted, the police may ask if you'll consent to a forensic rape examination (also called a "rape kit"). Forensic exams are used to collect evidence of sexual assault, such as the predator's DNA, and are vital to successfully prosecute criminal cases. DNA can be linked to your perpetrator through the FBI's national database.

Going through a forensic exam may be the last thing you want to do, but it's important for three reasons: (1) The evidence collected in your case may help police identify and capture the offender, which may protect others from being assaulted too. (2) You may decide to press charges later. This exam can be a powerful tool to help bring the predator to justice. (3) It's also imperative that you be tested for sexually transmitted diseases and that you know what your choices are regarding the prevention of a possible pregnancy.

While any doctor or nurse can perform the examination by following the instructions provided in the rape kit, some hospitals have specially trained personnel on staff called Sexual Assault Forensic Examiners (SAFEs) or Sexual Assault Nurse Examiners (SANEs). Research shows that programs with trained examiners increase evidence collection and investigation in sexual assault cases, which results in significantly higher prosecution rates. Further, SANEs and SAFEs are trained to conduct exams that are sensitive, dignified, and reduce trauma.

The forensic exam can take several hours to perform and it's important to remember that at any time you can ask to stop, pause, or skip a step. It's entirely your choice. This isn't a fun experience, but your courage in this moment could save other women and girls from being hurt by the same predator.

The Exam Process

Below is the general process for the forensic rape exam:

HISTORY

You'll be asked about your current medications, pre-existing conditions, and other questions about your health history. Some of the questions, such as those about recent consensual sexual activity, may seem very personal, but they're designed to ensure that DNA and other evidence collected from the exam can be connected to the perpetrator. You'll also be asked about the details of what happened to you to help identify all potential areas of injury, as well as places on your body or clothes where evidence may be located.

HEAD TO TOE EXAMINATION

This part of the exam may be based on your specific experience, which is why it's important to give an accurate history. Below are details of what the exam may entail, provided by End the Backlog:[lxxiv]

- The victim stands on a large sheet of paper while undressing in order to catch any hair or fiber evidence that may fall from her body. The victim's clothing and the sheet are collected for the testing of hair, fibers, and any additional evidence.
- During the physical exam, any injuries from the attack are documented and treated, and evidence is collected.
- The examiner collects biological evidence; such as saliva, blood, semen, urine, skin cells, and hair by taking swabs of the victim's skin, genitalia, anus, and mouth; scraping under the victim's fingernails; and combing through the victim's hair.
- The victim's body is photographed from head to toe to preserve evidence of bruising and injuries.

It's important to reiterate that any or all parts of this examination can be declined at any point.

When the forensic exam is complete, the evidence is carefully packaged and labeled to prevent contamination. (*Note: There's a nationwide backlog of rape kits, so be prepared for it to take weeks to months for your kit to be processed. Unfortunately, life just isn't like on TV crime shows where evidence is processed within minutes. And, if police don't feel they have enough evidence to proceed with an investigation or you choose not to make a report, the kit may not be processed at all.*)

Possible Mandatory Reporting

If you are a minor, the person performing the exam may be obligated to report it to law enforcement. You can learn more about mandatory reporting laws in your state through RAINN.org's State Law Database.

An Additional Option

Going through a forensic rape examination can be tough, but it's nowhere near as hard as enduring the rape. As difficult as it is, the rape exam is so important to the potential resolution of your case. Again, by getting the exam, you may save others from being harmed by the same perpetrator.

Having said that, if you absolutely are unwilling or emotionally unable to undergo a forensic rape exam, consider gathering your own evidence and storing it in plastic bags, including the clothing and undergarments you were wearing at the time of the incident; samples taken with cotton swabs of your mouth, vagina and/or rectum; photographs of any injuries; and a detailed written or recorded version of events. Sometimes bruises may not show up for a day or two, so if you do have injuries, photograph them each day until they disappear.

Store these items in a safe place, perhaps with a trusted friend or family member, or, better yet, your attorney. While these items may not have evidentiary value in court, police may later use them to link your case to a potential suspect.

Be sure to get follow-up medical care to identify, prevent and/or treat sexually transmitted diseases (STDs) or pregnancy, as described in the next section.

Follow-Up Care

When you go to the emergency room or your doctor, you may be offered preventative treatment for STDs and other forms of care that require a follow up appointment with a medical professional. If you're concerned you might have gotten pregnant because of the assault, ask about your reproductive options (for example, the "morning after" pill that prevents pregnancy if taken right after insemination). You don't have to take advantage of them, but it's good to know that you do have those options.

Depending on the circumstances and where you live, the examiner may schedule a follow-up appointment, or you can ask about resources in your community that offer follow-up care for survivors of sexual assault, such as Planned Parenthood and your local rape crisis center. Someone from the exam site may also be able to provide information or resources about your reporting options.

If you already have an established healthcare network in place, call your primary care physician and obstetrician to update your health records and get a full examination. Ensure you're tested for a full panel of sexually transmitted diseases, along with follow-up visits at recommended intervals. It's common to get tested for STDs such as HIV one to six months after the initial exam. (Most states have Victim Compensation funds that pay for costs incurred as the result of a crime. Check with your state's Attorney General's Office or ask your local rape crisis center if your state offers this program.)

You might find that it takes even longer for your sexual health to return to normal. It's not uncommon to have a series of abnormal pap smears after an assault. Talk with your doctor about the mid- and long-term effects of the assault and ask him or her when you should call for further support.

Coming Up Next...

In Chapter 13, you'll learn all about how the criminal justice process works and how to navigate the system. I include tips for testifying that will help you feel more confident on the stand. I'll even cover how to sue the perpetrator in civil court.

CHAPTER 13

Navigating the Criminal Justice Process

Going to Court

EVEN IF YOU choose to press charges against the perpetrator, the District Attorney's (DA's) Office ultimately decides whether to criminally prosecute the case. If they don't think their case is strong enough (i.e., there's not enough evidence for a conviction), they may choose to drop the charges. This can be very upsetting for survivors who've endured significant emotional turmoil to get to this point.

Don't despair; you can still bring a civil suit against your assailant, which I'll talk about below. First, let's assume the DA has decided to prosecute your case. What does the process look like?

MEETING WITH THE PROSECUTOR

The DA's Office will handle the prosecution of your case. To be clear, they are not *your* attorney; they represent the "state." The DA has a staff of attorneys, called prosecutors, who manage his cases. Unless it's a high-profile case, you're unlikely to meet with the DA himself. You'll meet with an Assistant District Attorney and/or investigator who will conduct a thorough interview with you to determine the facts of the case.

It may be difficult to tell your story to a stranger, but that's part of the process, and it's good practice for when you testify in court. Tell the truth of what you remember to the best of your ability. If you don't know the answer to a question, don't make one up to please the prosecutor. It's better to admit you don't know than to guess and be accused of lying later in court. You can ask for a copy of your statement before the case goes to trial to refresh your memory.

COURT APPEARANCES AND HEARINGS

Before the actual trial, there may be several court appearances where they formally charge the offender and/or a grand jury hearing. A grand jury is a closed event where the prosecutor lays out the basic evidence of the case to a judge or small jury in order to obtain an indictment (a determination that there's a factual basis for criminal charges). The perpetrator, now called the "defendant," usually isn't present at this event and you may not be required to testify or be present.

If the prosecutor decides to file a felony complaint rather than present the case to a grand jury, the defendant is entitled to a preliminary hearing. At that hearing, the prosecutor must show that there's enough evidence to warrant a trial.

Additional hearings will be held and motions will likely be made in the months preceding the trial as the prosecution and defense teams attempt to enter or suppress evidence and witnesses. You won't usually need to be present at these hearings. The prosecutor will keep you apprised of any action required on your part.

Delays and trial date postponements are common, so don't be surprised if the date of the trial changes several times, sometimes months later than originally planned.

GET EDUCATED

Learn as much as you can about the case, such as the exact charges; the names of the prosecutor, defense attorney, and judge; and whether there's a victim advocate assigned to your case (if not, ask for one). Ask the prosecutor to meet with you before you testify.

Find out if the DA plans to offer a plea deal to the defendant and, if so, what the deal is. A plea deal is a lighter sentence a prosecutor offers the defendant in exchange for his guilty plea. This saves the "state" (which is doing the prosecuting) time and money, and helps them get a win if they aren't sure there's enough evidence to get a conviction. You won't have to testify if a plea deal is reached. It's up to the prosecutor and the DA whether they offer a plea deal or not. Although your opinion may be taken into consideration, they have the final say.

Before meeting with anyone on the prosecution's team, it's a good idea to write down your questions and thoughts so you don't forget them. Keep careful notes in a journal so you can refer to them before you testify. This will increase your confidence that you're on top of things.

Ask the prosecutor or victim advocate to give you a tour of the courtroom before your court date so you know who sits where and you don't feel intimidated on the day of the trial.

DEALING WITH THE MEDIA

By law, the media can't disclose the names of sexual assault victims, so unless you choose to reveal your name to them, they can't include it in their reports. This doesn't guarantee no one will find out who you are; people do talk and word gets around, but at least you shouldn't have your name bandied about in the newspapers and on TV.

ABOUT THE JUDGE AND JURY

If your case is going to a jury trial, the prosecution and defense teams need to agree on the selection of 12 men and women they believe will be impartial when considering the facts of the case. Remember that the defendant is considered *innocent until proven guilty beyond a reasonable doubt.* "Guilty beyond a reasonable doubt" means all 12 jurors agree that the prosecution adequately proved the offender committed the crime. They're tasked with basing their decision on reason or common sense, not assumptions, sympathy, or prejudice.

Testifying: The Prosecution

The first day of court may be the first time since the assault that you see the perpetrator and his family and friends if the case involved an assault by a stranger. If it's someone you know, maybe even someone you loved, it can be unnerving to face him down. Be sure you're surrounded by friends and family of your own who can offer support and encouragement. Your local rape crisis center may be able to send one of their advocates to sit with you throughout the process to provide additional support.

It's important to note that you likely will not be allowed to be present in the courtroom during the trial, with the exception of your time on the witness stand when you're testifying against the perpetrator. The prosecutor's office will be able to tell you if and when you can sit in on the proceedings. Family members and friends who aren't testifying may be able to observe the trial and can keep you informed of what's happening.

If you believe you can't testify in front of your assailant, ask the prosecutor if you can testify on closed-circuit TV. You'll still have to answer the defense attorney's questions, but you won't have to do so while your offender stares you down. This may not be granted, but you can at least ask.

The prosecution always goes first in court and the defense second. Both sides make opening statements which may contain very strong accusations against you and/or the defendant. As difficult as it is, you must remain quiet and maintain your composure throughout the process, regardless of any mistakes or incorrect accusations the defense attorney makes about you. Speaking out when you're not on the stand is not allowed and may make you look less credible.

If the defense attorney says something you know isn't true, write a note to the prosecutor (the attorney representing your case) to point it out. Work to appear calm and impartial, no matter what's happening.

Next, the prosecutor will call her witnesses to the stand, including you, to give testimony before the judge and jury. The spotlight will be on you, but know that it's the prosecutor's job to make you feel comfortable and to help you tell your story in a logical fashion. She'll begin by asking you simple questions, such as your name and where you live, until you start to relax and become more comfortable with the line of questioning. Next, she'll lead you on a step by step progression through your memories of the crime. Just listen to her carefully and answer each question as it comes. She's not going to try to confuse you or make you look bad.[lxxv]

Take your time telling your story. It's normal to be nervous, even terrified. If you get upset and start to cry on the stand, that's okay. Ask for tissues, breathe deeply a few times, and continue your testimony when you can.[lxxvi] If you need a drink of water or time to collect yourself, ask the judge if you can take a short break. If you start to feel overwhelmed, remind yourself that you're doing this to secure justice for yourself and to ensure the defendant doesn't victimize anyone else.

Marie De Santis of the Women's Justice Center advises survivors to make a list before they have to testify of all the things they're most afraid will happen in court. Ask the prosecutor or victim advocate what will happen if those things actually occur. Most of the time, they'll be able to reassure you that such questions aren't allowed. De Santis reminds survivors to remember they're not the ones on trial. If you're asked a tough question, such as whether you lied to police about using drugs the night of the attack, be honest. It's better to calmly say, "Yes, I lied to the police because I didn't think they would believe me about the rape if I told them I was using drugs," than to get flustered and defensive.[lxxvii]

It may help to remember that the perpetrator is *terrified* of you; you hold the key to his cage, so to speak, and he's worried you'll prevail in court. Use that knowledge to empower yourself to speak your truth with confidence. You may even find the process of telling your story to be cathartic, releasing some or all of the power the perpetrator holds in your mind.

Testifying: The Defense

Now it's the defense's turn to question you. The defender's job is to convince the jury that his client is innocent of the charges against him, and he'll use all means at his disposal to strengthen his case, including trying to paint you as a bad person, possibly even a liar trying to harm his client with false testimony. Don't worry; the prosecutor will be listening to him carefully so she can jump in to object to any false or inflammatory statements.

The defense attorney may try to rattle you while you're on the stand, asking probing questions designed to throw you off your story. He may appear friendly one minute and accusatory at the next. His job is to make you stumble and to say something that's not in your police or investigator's statement so he can shake the jury's confidence in you and your claim. Keep reminding yourself to BREATHE while you're on the stand. Continue to go at your own pace, taking as much time as you need to answer his questions.

The defense attorney may try to find small inconsistencies in your testimony, such as "Five minutes ago you said the defendant had on glasses and now you say he didn't." Don't let this type of questioning upset you. It's just a desperate attempt by the defense to make you feel confused. Correct yourself if you need to and offer an explanation only if you have to.

You can (and should) tell the prosecutor and defense attorney immediately if you don't understand a question, and you can turn to the judge and ask if you are required to answer a particular question. Some defense attorneys will ask inappropriate questions that aren't allowed—about things like your past sexual history, whether you've used drugs in the past, etc., knowing the prosecutor is likely to object. He'll try to ask these questions anyway hoping to get you to act guilty and defensive in front of the jury. Don't fall for it![lxxviii]

If you can allow yourself to see the defense attorney as just another guy doing his job, it might help you be more patient and composed under questioning. Remember, if you don't recall the answer to a question or you feel confused, just admit it and make the attorney move to the next question.

TIPS FOR WHEN YOU'RE TESTIFYING

The Rape, Abuse & Incest National Network (RAINN.org) offers the following tips to help you stay focused and calm when you take the stand:[lxxix]

- Allow yourself to take brief pauses. If, at any time, you're feeling overwhelmed, ask the judge or prosecutor for a short break.
- Stay hydrated; bring a water bottle and take sips of water throughout.
- If you feel yourself getting angry or frustrated, take a moment to pause. Breathe deeply several times to regain your composure.

- Keep your eyes focused on the person asking you questions, rather than looking at the perpetrator or his supporters.
- Always tell the truth. If you don't remember something exactly, it's important to say so. If you say something you didn't mean to, or you think something came across in a way you didn't intend, you can clarify your statement. Ask the judge, "May I go back to something I previously said?"
- This is important: Answer the questions—and nothing more. Don't volunteer additional information unless you're asked.
- Every trial is different. If you have specific questions about testifying, check in with the prosecuting attorney or victim advocate.

Closing Arguments and Jury Deliberations

After all the witnesses (including you) have been questioned, the state (prosecutor) and defense will rest their cases. Now it's time for closing arguments. Once again, the defense attorney will attempt to paint you as an unreliable witness at best, and a liar at worst.

Now the case goes to the jury for deliberations and a decision, which may take anywhere from a few hours to several days. Possible outcomes include:

- **A guilty verdict**, which means all 12 jurors decided the defendant was guilty of his crime and will be sentenced by the judge immediately or at a future date.

- **An innocent verdict** means all 12 jurors agreed the defendant was not guilty of the crime. Upon announcement of the "not guilty" verdict, the person is no longer in custody and is free to go. Due to double jeopardy laws, the offender can't be tried twice for the same crime if he's found innocent.

- **A "mistrial" or "hung jury"** means the 12 jurors couldn't agree on whether the defendant was innocent or guilty based on the facts presented. Even if 11 of the 12 people agree on his guilt, a mistrial will be declared if the 12th juror doesn't change her vote of innocence. At this point, the prosecutor may elect to completely drop the case or she may choose to retry the case with another jury.

Sentencing

Sentencing may be handed down by the judge immediately, or a sentencing date may be set weeks or months in the future. That doesn't necessarily mean the convicted predator (now a felon) goes free until then; it's most likely he'll go to jail until his prison sentence is announced.

Before determining the sentence, the judge may hear arguments by the defense for a minimal sentence and by the prosecution for the stiffest sentence possible. In many states, survivors can offer a victim impact statement, in person or in writing, expressing the impact the crime and offender have had on their lives and the lives of their family. The victim impact statement may argue for a greater or lighter sentence, which the judge will consider when making her decision.

The Appeals Process

After a conviction, the felon has the right to file an appeal against his conviction. He may also apply for bail (release) while waiting for a ruling on his appeal. The prosecutor's office should notify you if an appeal has been filed and inform you of any hearings so you can be present to testify if needed.

Many states now have automated victim notification systems that enable you to sign up to receive phone calls or texts if your offender is to be released from custody so you can take precautions for your safety, if necessary. Ask the prosecutor or victim advocate if such a system exists in your state.

Suing the Perpetrator in Civil Court

Whether the perpetrator is found innocent or guilty, you have the right to sue him in civil court where monetary damages may be awarded. The verdict here is based on the less demanding "preponderance of the evidence," meaning the jurors (or judge) agree that it's more likely than not the crime was committed by the defendant. You will have to hire your own attorney to prosecute your case in civil court, which may be costly.

According to the National Crime Victim Bar Association, the civil justice system doesn't attempt to determine the innocence or guilt of an offender, and offenders are also not put in prison if you win the civil suit. Civil courts only determine whether an offender or a third party is liable for the injuries sustained because of the crime.[lxxx]

Civil suits are another way to punish the defendant for his actions and allow for damages for things like compensatory damages, such as emotional distress, lost wages, and medical bills; nominal damages for injuries whose affect can't be measured; and punitive damages, which are awarded for actions that are especially malicious or oppressive.

SUING THIRD PARTIES

You may also sue other individuals or companies that failed to adequately maintain property or provide security, or who were negligent in the hiring or retention of employees.[lxxxi] Examples include landlords who don't provide sufficient lighting on their premises, businesses that don't provide adequate security, schools that fail to protect students, and churches that don't fire abusive priests.

Your spouse can even file a "consortium claim" for intentional infliction of the emotional distress he or she had to deal with in the aftermath of the crime. For example, your spouse may claim that as a result of your post-traumatic stress, the two of you can no longer have sex or maintain a healthy relationship.

COMING UP NEXT...

Post-Traumatic Stress Disorder (PTSD) is common after a violent assault. In the next chapter, I'll talk about life in the aftermath, and help you understand what PTSD is and how it manifests so you can seek the help you need.

CHAPTER 14

Life in the Aftermath

PEOPLE WHO HAVEN'T experienced a traumatic event, like sexual assault, may wrongly assume that once the crime is over, life goes back to normal. The fact is, your life will never go back to the way it was before the assault. But know that you'll find your "new normal" and can go on to live a happy—even joyful—life. I did it, so can you.

The Purpose of Shame and Fear

I once heard that guilt is: "I did something wrong." Shame is: "There's something wrong with *me*." If you're feeling ashamed of what happened, that means you're blaming yourself in some way. Shame is an emotion generated by your inner cop—the part of your mind that polices your thoughts and actions to help keep you safe. But sometimes our inner cop runs amok and becomes our judge, jury, and executioner.

Maybe you did play "doctor" with your older brother when you were a kid. Maybe you did flirt with that guy or let him get to third base. Maybe you enjoyed the attention of your friend's father. Maybe you went jogging at night alone despite your friend's warnings that it was dangerous. So what? Your behavior was NOT an invitation to rape you or beat you or stalk you!

Feel those words deep in your bones and embrace their truth. Once you recognize that fact, you can let go of the shame because it doesn't belong to you; it belongs to **him**. Give it back to him now.

Even fear has an important purpose—to warn you of potential or actual danger. It's there to protect you; but it, too, can run amok, making you hypervigilant and afraid of every noise and shadow. I'll talk about post-traumatic stress disorder below and how it inhibits our ability to move on from the trauma.

What You Can Count On

You should expect to enjoy the freedom of living your life without the fear of being assaulted. That women can't always do that is a sad reality. The fact is, the world isn't fair and it doesn't owe you anything. The only thing you can count on is your own inner strength.

You may find you can't even count on the support of your friends and family after you've become a "victim." They may not want to believe you, or they may even blame you and try to shame you. While it's easy to embrace the victim mentality and buy into their projections (and that's all they are, projections of their fear and ignorance onto you), you must fight that urge and stand on your own two feet.

You were the target of a crime; that's a fact. But it doesn't say *anything* about who you are at your core or in your spirit.

Like a major earthquake, trauma has psychological and physical aftershocks that continue to rock us long after the initial catastrophe. These are discussed below.

The Psychological Aftermath

There's no "right way" to react after you've been the victim of a crime. Some people go into shock and feel completely dissociated from the event; they may appear calm and unemotional. Others become very emotional and can't stop thinking about what happened.

Some degree of shock is common, which can impair your thinking and ability to react "appropriately" afterward. Because you may not be able to feel or recall the trauma at first, you might downplay the event or be confused about what really happened. Other people remember every detail and are completely overwhelmed by the emotions and sensations, which can be paralyzing.

After being raped at 19, I became so dissociated that I literally have no memory of the two months following the incident. I flunked out of school that semester and when I did come back to reality, I turned immediately to self-blame to bring some sense of order to my universe.

It sounds counter-intuitive, but people who've been traumatized often seek balance and control—sometimes including self-blame and punishment—to regain equilibrium. They don't want to accept that they were vulnerable and powerless to stop their predator; it's easier to blame themselves for "stupid" behavior than to accept that they live in a world where such a soul-shattering thing could happen to them.

Self-loathing and shame can run so deep in survivors that it may take years before they ever tell anyone, if they tell at all. A few years ago, I met an elderly woman, around 80 years old, who came up to me after I gave a presentation to whisper in my ear that she had been raped by her brother when she was 14 and had never told a soul. I whispered back, "You just did," and she smiled.

Survivors often believe that if others could see how damaged and flawed they are, other people—especially those closest to them—would run from them in disgust and horror.

Post-Traumatic Stress Disorder

Most people have heard of Post-Traumatic Stress Disorder, known as PTSD, as it relates to men and women who fought in combat. But PTSD is an equal opportunity condition—it can affect survivors of any kind of trauma, from violence to natural disasters, and from car accidents to severe childhood physical and emotional neglect.

PTSD is a mental health condition triggered by experiencing or witnessing a terrifying event. Symptoms may include flashbacks, nightmares, and severe anxiety, as well as uncontrollable thoughts about the event.

Many people go through traumatic events and may have difficulty adjusting and coping for a period of time, but they don't have PTSD; with time, support, and good self-care, they usually get better. PTSD is generally diagnosed when the symptoms get worse, last for months or years, and interfere with your ability to function.[lxxxii]

Symptoms of PTSD

People with PTSD experience symptoms that impair their ability to live a normal, emotionally healthy life. Reminders of the event can trigger panic attacks or make you feel you're emotionally out of control. For me, before I recovered from the trauma, sex with my first husband was like reliving the rape every time. My reaction to his advances and my emotional state constantly caused problems in our relationship and we ended up divorcing.

One study found that over half of survivors who were forcibly raped while under the influence of alcohol or drugs developed lifetime PTSD. These victims were also almost five times more likely to have lifetime major depressive episodes than non-victims. Survivors of sexual assault are also more likely than non-victims to engage in risky behavior, such as substance and alcohol abuse, smoking, and high-risk HIV behavior.[lxxxiii]

People of any age can get PTSD, but some are more likely to experience it if they have other factors in play, such as experiencing long-lasting trauma, having a history of childhood abuse or neglect, being in a job that exposes them to trauma (like combat or accident scenes), having existing mental health problems like depression or anxiety, or not having a good support system of friends and family.

According to the Mayo Clinic,[lxxxiv] additional symptoms of PTSD include:

INTRUSIVE MEMORIES OF THE EVENT(S), SUCH AS:

- Recurring, unwanted, and distressing memories.
- Flashbacks that cause you to relive the event, which can be triggered by certain sights, sounds, smells, or people.
- Upsetting dreams.
- Severe emotional distress or physical reactions to things that remind you of the event.

AVOIDANCE:

- Trying to avoid thinking or talking about the traumatic event.
- Avoiding people, places, and activities that remind you of the event.

CHANGES IN THINKING AND MOOD:

- Negative feelings about yourself or other people.
- Inability to experience positive emotions.
- Feeling emotionally numb.
- Hopelessness about the future.
- Memory problems, including memories of the event.
- Difficulty maintaining close relationships.

CHANGES IN EMOTIONAL REACTIONS:

- Irritability, angry outbursts, or aggressive behavior.
- Being constantly on guard for danger (hypervigilance).
- Overwhelming guilt or shame.
- Self-destructive behavior, such as abusing drugs or alcohol, cutting one's self, etc.
- Being easily startled or frightened.
- Trouble concentrating.
- Trouble sleeping.

- Suicidal thinking or suicide attempts. (If you have suicidal thoughts, please see the Appendix at the end of this book to find an agency that can help you deal with that.)

In addition to the symptoms of PTSD, survivors may experience other physical, social, and sexual problems, such as serious injuries, pregnancy, or sexually transmitted diseases as a direct result of their assaults. Later, they may develop eating disorders, insomnia, trouble maintaining healthy relationships, or sexual problems that require medical intervention.

According to the National Crime Victimization Survey:[lxxxv]

- **Women who are raped** or stalked by any perpetrator, or who are physically assaulted by an intimate partner are more likely to have asthma, irritable bowel syndrome, and diabetes, and are also more likely than non-victims to suffer from chronic pain, frequent headaches, and difficulty sleeping.
- **Survivors of sexual assault** are more likely to smoke, to have high cholesterol and hypertension, and to be obese.
- **African American women** ages 18-24 who are sexually assaulted are nearly five times more likely to test positive for a high-risk Human Papillomavirus (HPV) infection.
- **Survivors of intimate partner rape** or sexual assault are more likely than non-victims to contract sexually-transmitted infections, and are also more likely to report HIV risk factors, such as unprotected sex, injection drug use, and alcohol abuse.

The News Isn't All Bad

I shared a lot of information in this chapter, and you may feel overwhelmed. It's critical to recognize that there's so much support and so many resources in your community and around the country to help you work through the aftermath of your experience. (Some of these are shared in the Appendix.)

It's so important that you know that what happened was NOT your fault and that you possess the strength and courage to find your new normal and move on to have a wonderful life.

COMING UP NEXT...

In the final chapter, I share my story of how I triumphed over PTSD and a resulting life-threatening medical condition after I sought help. You'll learn the greatest piece of advice I ever received that shook me from my self-induced victim trance, and forced me to confront my past and move forward toward healing.

CHAPTER 15

The Light at the End of the Trauma Tunnel

Life isn't made up of the things that happened to you.

It's how you choose to move forward that matters.

―――◦◦◦◦―――

It's Not Your Fault!

NO MATTER WHAT happened or whether or not you fought back against the perpetrator, the most important thing to remember is that *the attack was not your fault* and that you survived! The perpetrator is the one who chose to commit a crime and chose you, for whatever reason, as his target. There was nothing you did to deserve such treatment.

I spent decades blaming myself—for "looking too pretty," for going into my date's apartment, for believing the lies of people who chose to exploit me. I suffered terrible mental anguish over the years before I accepted that I was renting those predators space in my head. They didn't deserve to be there in that sacred space, so I kicked their asses out! Granted, it took a lot of therapy and time reading self-help books, but I made it through the trauma and found an amazing life on the other side.

How I Came to Grips with the Trauma

Like many survivors, I was high-functioning, despite what had happened to me as a child and teenager. I managed to "fake it till I made it" and was rapidly climbing the career ladder to success. In secret, though, I suffered from severe anxiety, constant digestive problems, and extreme self-loathing.

(Again, if you are not completely in love with yourself, if you have any shred of self-loathing and believe that you're inherently flawed in some way, I encourage you to read my short story, Escape from the Terrible Garden, *which appears at the very end of this book.)*

Over the years, as the stress piled up, I eventually became severely ill and was diagnosed with two life-threatening auto-immune diseases (lupus and scleroderma). Now I was struggling against both mind and body to keep my world from spinning out of control.

WHEN EVERYTHING FELL APART

Then, one day when I was 29, I was sitting in a board meeting of community leaders and without warning I burst into tears! I fled to the bathroom and huddled in a stall. I sobbed there for two hours without being able to tell my very concerned co-workers what was going on. I couldn't tell them because I frankly had no clue myself why I was crying.

Within a week, I was sitting in front of a therapist at the local rape crisis center. Telling the story of my childhood molestations and teenage rapes to this stranger took every ounce of courage I had. After the words poured out, I hung my head and waited to be judged. Instead, the therapist touched my hand gently and said, "I'm so sorry that happened to you. It wasn't your fault."

At first, I rejected her comforting words. Maybe she didn't hear me correctly. But she had heard me perfectly and said exactly what I needed to hear. With her help and that of a group of other rape survivors, I began to look differently at what happened. I was urged to shift the blame to the perpetrators where it belonged. But still I resisted, clinging to that stubborn need to blame myself.

PUTTING IT ALL TOGETHER

It wasn't until I heard a woman in my therapy group share her story of how she had been brutally raped under circumstances similar to mine that I began to get it. I felt so angry about what had happened to her! I could see so clearly that it wasn't her fault. Then it struck me—if it wasn't her fault and I felt angry about what happened to *her*, then maybe it wasn't my fault either!

I could feel things rapidly shifting in my mind as I recognized that not only was I *not* to blame for what happened to me, but that I had the right to feel angry about it—and boy, did I get mad! For a while there I was a bundle of rage and vengeance. I saw the world through a red filter that made every man look like a predator (sorry guys!) and I copped an attitude of defiance. In my dreams, I fought furiously with faceless predators. One night, I woke up in a heap on the floor of my bedroom after I had lunged in my dream to attack a predator who was trying to assault a child. Fortunately, I passed through that phase without physically injuring anyone (or myself).

I had identified myself as a victim for so many years that when I finally identified myself as a "survivor," I wore it like a badge of honor. After decades of stifling myself, I felt compelled to blurt out my story and told almost everyone I ran into, strangers included, that I was a survivor of abuse. As inappropriate as I may have been, it felt empowering to claim my story and declare my battle scars to the world. This phase, too, eventually passed.

PHYSICAL BREAKDOWN

But my physical symptoms persisted. By 2000, I was so ill from the lupus and scleroderma that I had to stop working. I was so debilitated from swollen and painful joints that I couldn't turn a doorknob or hold a coffee cup; I had to crawl up the stairs on my hands and knees. In 2002 my rheumatologist told me my heart was failing and that it could stop at any time. I dove back into a deep depression and waited for the end.

Then I was offered the opportunity to meet with a Tibetan Buddhist lama for advice. I hobbled up to his house, made a pitiful bow and burst into tears. I poured out my tale of woe and waited for him to shower me with sympathy. And that's when I learned that lamas don't do dramas! Instead, he gave me a cosmic bitch slap, commanding me to "stop feeling sorry for myself and start thinking about the happiness of others."

I was shocked! I was offended! Didn't he realize I was *dying*? Help others? I couldn't even help myself! But the lama was insistent. On the drive home, I wondered what I could possibly do to help others in my debilitated state. At that moment, an ambulance passed by with the siren blaring and I said a quick wish that the person inside would find help and healing. I thought, "I can do that!" and began sending good wishes to the drivers around me.

DISCOVERING THE SECRET TO HAPPINESS

Then one day I was at the mall on my scooter and saw an elderly woman struggling to walk. I gave her my cane and felt a small flush of happiness. So I did more, letting the mom with the crying baby go ahead of me in line at the grocery store, picking up trash on the sidewalk, putting inspirational notes on the driver's side door of cars at the cancer center. I began to make it a practice to perform at least one act of kindness each day. And I felt happier.

What I didn't know at the time, was that science has proven that when we help others, we get a dose of mood-boosting serotonin and pain-killing endorphins. So every time I did something kind, I was literally healing my body from the inside-out. I had spent so many years focused solely on my own pain and suffering, that I neglected to see that everyone had a story and was fighting a hard battle. Performing those acts of kindness reconnected me with my humanity and the suffering of others, and made me more compassionate and grateful.

I reached a point where I was so happy and so filled with gratitude that it no longer mattered whether I was sick or ill, or even living or dying. I was filled with joy and accepted every moment as a gift. I realized that the traumas I had endured didn't define me; they were only things that happened to me a long time ago. I came to fall in love with my wonderful, perfectly flawed Self.

I realized, too, that I could *choose* to let go of my story, to let go of the fear and anger and victim mentality. I saw that I could choose happiness. It was at that point that my condition went into remission! I feel better today than I have in decades.

What's YOUR Story?

The point of telling you my story was to give you a sense of hope that there is a light at the end of the trauma tunnel and maybe to inspire you to see your story in a new way.

You may not be there today or tomorrow or the day after that, but you *will* get there if you choose to let loose your inner badass and lean on your support network (family, friends, therapist, group therapy friends). Just because you blame yourself doesn't mean you will forever. Just because you were hurt doesn't mean you'll hurt for all time.

If your trauma occurred recently, this might seem impossible. It's okay. Your world has just been blown to bits; give yourself a break and know you're doing the best you can. I urge you to seek individual and group counseling, which saved my life and can move you safely through the healing process.

If the incident happened long ago, think about whether you're ready to let it go and move forward to live life on *your* terms.

It's time.

A Note to My Readers

BELOW IS A short story I wrote nearly 30 years ago, when I still lived with the belief that there was something inherently wrong with me that made good people do bad things. I was so filled with shame and self-loathing then, and believed that no one could possible understand or love me.

If you share any of these feelings, I urge you to read *Escape from the Terrible Garden* that follows, and know that you are NOT alone.

I am building an online tribe of women and girls, and creating a safe space where we can meet and share our experiences, our advice, and our support for one another. Men are welcome to join another group I'm starting that is dedicated to stopping sexual violence against both genders. For more information, visit my website at www.cjscarlet.com or contact me at cj@cjscarlet.com.

May you have perfect peace and healing. Love, CJ

Escape from the Terrible Garden

by CJ Scarlet

To all those who beckoned me along the path.

———

ONCE UPON A *time . . .*

In the darkest corner of the deepest black hole in the universe, where the souls of deeply wounded children hide from their tormentors, there was a terrible garden.

In that garden lived a wretched young woman with a hideous disease. On the outside, to the rest of the world, the young woman appeared strong and healthy. She went to work every day and took care of her young sons every night. She smiled sweetly and did as she was told, all the while terrified that when she spoke maggots would fall from her mouth, or that when she reached to shake someone's hand a snake would slither from her sleeve.

She lived in constant fear that her disease, which somehow made good people do bad things, would contaminate those around her, especially the people she loved.

For years and years she managed to fool everybody. But all the time she was acting fine for the outside world, pretending like she lived there, she was secretly trapped in the terrible garden.

In that cursed place, everything was shrouded in a thick, evil fog that made it hard for the young woman to see or hear anything clearly. Vines, rising in twisted coils around lifeless trees, formed a canopy that blocked all sunlight and warmth from above. The boggy soil teemed with misshapen creatures that fought over decaying corpses that littered the ground.

The young woman had lived there so long she was no longer bothered by the bitter, rotting stench that permeated the entire garden; it was as sweet to her as lilacs.

What a horrible place! you say. *Why would anyone choose to live in such a garden?!* you ask. Ah, but the young woman with the hideous disease believed her garden to be the most perfect on earth. For in her terrible garden she felt *safe*.

She knew the slimy, slithering beasts around her by name, and they knew all her shameful secrets. In fact, she believed she was even *lower* and *more terrible* than the creatures around her, so she was grateful for their companionship and for the bare existence she found there.

Day and night she tended her garden, nurturing the stunted, thorny stalks, thankful for the pain they offered. Anxiously she yanked out anything that threatened to hurt her senses with their violent reds and purples and greens.

She attempted to escape once, years ago, to try to live fully in the outside world. But as she struggled to climb through the vines – just as she stretched her hand into the sunlight – the creatures began to scream her secrets. And so, terrified that the world would hear her shame and see the ghastly scars on her body and realize just how hideous she really was, she allowed the vines to pull her back into their soothing, numbing embrace.

She tried to be happy again in her garden. Really, she did. But her hand – the one that had touched the sun – would not stop burning. The pain of it was different from any pain she had ever known. It did not sear her insides the way the secrets did, and it did not sting her skin like the thorns.

No, this was different, and it bothered her very much. This pain was like a deep, ancient *ache*. And for some reason, whenever that hand stroked her children's hair or caressed their little faces, it made her heart hurt and her throat swell. She tried not to touch anyone with that hand for fear they would be forever scarred.

Something was wrong with her; she just knew it. The burning in her hand must be the shame finally consuming her. "Thank God," she thought. "Finally, this hurting will end." She prepared herself to die the fiery death she had prayed for all her life. All that was left to do was to say goodbye to her children.

She slipped into their darkened room late one night and bent low to kiss the cheek on her eldest child. "Goodbye, my love," she whispered, leaving a tear where her kiss had been.

She turned to the baby, sleeping softly in his crib. For a moment she forgot herself and allowed her hand to brush a curl from his tiny forehead. The baby smiled in his sleep. She snatched her hand away and peered anxiously where her touch had lingered. No mark was left, thank heaven.

"How is it," she wondered, "that my touch has never burned my sons and that they have not been contaminated by my disease?"

The vines in her garden rasped, "Don't worry. When they get older, they too will come to live in our terrible garden."

These words tore through the young woman's heart like a vicious claw, and very nearly killed her right then and there. Unable to bear the thought that her precious sons – the two beings she loved more than life itself – would be forever relegated to the terrible garden because of her, the young woman decided that for their sakes she would try just once more to escape.

Dashing the tears from her eyes, she summoned her courage and began to climb through the vines. As they slipped their twisted coils tighter and tighter around her, she thought they would squeeze the very breath from her body. She tore at them with her hands and, to her amazement, they fell away – withered by the touch of her burning hand.

With renewed determination, she climbed higher and higher, ignoring the thorns that pierced her skin and the creatures that tore at her hair. She was so close to the light she could reach out her hand and feel its glow once more.

But then she heard the dreadful, familiar wail as the creatures began to shriek her shame to the outside world. She froze, paralyzed by indecision. She had come so far and was so close to escaping, but she knew that the humiliation she would suffer at the hands of the outsiders once they knew her secrets would be too devastating to endure. What was she to do?

The shrieking and moaning grew louder and louder. She covered her ears with her hands to try to shut out the noise. But it grew louder and louder still. She began to scream too, hoping to drown it out, and she started to feel dizzy and very crazy.

Just when she thought the world would explode from the chaos, she heard a new noise, so faint it was almost imperceptible. In fact, at first she didn't hear it with her ears, she *felt* it – a faint reverberation in that same place where her heart hurt and her throat ached.

She stopped screaming and paused to listen. There it was again! --this time a distant sound that slipped through the shrieking.

It was. . . a *whisper.*

The more she concentrated on that one tiny sound, the more distant the shrieking seemed. Holding ever so still, more still than she had ever been in her life, she heard the whisper once more. It sounded like – her name! It was coming from outside! With rising excitement, the young woman tore through the upper canopy of vines and into the light.

There before her, leaning on the gnarled branch of a mossy, ancient oak, was an older woman with fine white hair and crinkly blue eyes. She reached out to take the young woman's hand, but the young woman shrank back, afraid her touch would burn the kind lady.

The older woman smiled and said, "Your touch will not hurt me."

"But it will," the young woman warned.

The older woman grabbed her hand tightly and said, "See, I am unharmed."

The young woman tried to pull away. "You don't understand!" she pleaded anxiously. "I have a hideous disease that makes good people do bad things. I have secrets that are so unspeakable they destroy everything they touch! Leave me alone before they destroy you too!" she begged.

But the older woman still smiled. "I know your secrets, and they don't scare me a bit."

The young woman looked at her in disbelief. *This is terrible,* she thought. *This poor, addled woman doesn't realize the danger she is in. If my disease doesn't kill her, she will surely hate me when she finds out how horrible my secrets really are! I've got to do something to save us both!*

So the young woman put on her most ferocious face and began to screech at the older woman, trying to frighten her away. She had used this trick many times in the past to protect those who got too close or cared too much, and it had always worked. She railed and screamed until her voice grew ragged and hoarse. She clawed at the skin on her own body, turning it inside out to reveal the roots of all her scars. She growled and bared her teeth like a feral animal.

But no matter what the young woman did, the older woman would not budge, and she would not let go of her hand. Finally, the young woman fell in an exhausted heap at the older woman's feet. "Who ARE you?" she sobbed. "What's WRONG with you? Why aren't you running away?"

The older woman knelt down and wrapped her arms around the young woman's quivering body, holding her very gently. "I am one of many, many people who care about you. I am here to help you take the very first step on a journey that will lead you from your terrible garden toward a life filled with peace and joy."

The young woman hardly dared to breathe. She hung on every word the older woman spoke, wanting desperately to believe her.

"You mean everything's okay? I won't have to go back to that terrible place ever again? I can be happy now?" she whispered hopefully.

The older woman sighed in a sad, wise way. "No, my dear, there is still much you must do to truly escape the terrible garden and begin to heal. But from now on, you will never have to return there alone. There will be others, like me, who will be at your side as you battle those dreadful creatures, to remind you how strong and brave and good you are."

"I think you must have mistaken me for someone else," the young woman sniffed sadly, hanging her head. "I am not any of those things. But . . . thank you for trying." She rose and began to walk dejectedly back toward the garden.

"Before you go," the older woman said, "I want to show you something." The young woman did not want to turn around. She liked this kind woman so much and she knew she would miss her once she was back in her terrible garden. But the young woman always did what she was told, so she turned to face the older woman.

She looked into her wise blue eyes and saw . . . hope? Life? Love! Joy, contentment, success, laughter, friendship!!

A flurry of emotions swept by – all *hers*. She saw herself as an old, wise woman with her tall, strong, loving sons by her side. The young woman saw all this and more that she would achieve in her life. She saw her future self – the one who was waiting for her to make the choice. The choice to live, to heal, to *be*.

And in that instant, the young woman knew she *was* strong and brave and good. She *could* make the journey!

As the older woman saw the wonder dawn in the young woman's eyes, she laughed with joy. "Someday," she said, "many years from now, you and I will meet again, and we'll rejoice in your victory. I'll be waiting for you." And with that, the older woman faded away.

"No!" the young woman cried. "Come back! I need you! I can't do this without you!" But the older woman had vanished. The young woman crumpled to the ground sobbing. She cried for a long time before she heard another whisper.

She leaped to her feet, expecting to see the older woman before her. Instead, to her surprise, she saw another woman, and behind her another woman, and another and another and another . . . all smiling and holding out their hands, beckoning her forward, encouraging her on her journey.

And waaaaay off in the distance, so many years in the future she could barely make her out, was the older woman, waiting. Just as she had promised.

The young woman smiled then, and took her first step.

The End

About the Author

CJ SCARLET KNOWS first-hand how violence can destroy lives. A survivor of childhood molestations and rape as a college freshman, CJ spent years dealing with the emotional aftermath of her experience. Then she took her power back and became an advocate for others who had been victimized.

Today CJ has a clear mission: to help women and girls live safer, more confident lives, backed by the knowledge that they can and must protect themselves. Through her books, video blogs, presentations, and corporate training programs, CJ shares her expertise to empower her "tribe" to take THEIR power back too.

While serving as Director of Victims Issues with the North Carolina Attorney General's Office, CJ initiated and co-chaired the implementation of the nation's first statewide automated victim notification system, selected as the national model, which contacts victims before their perpetrators are released from custody.

An expert in victims' rights and advocacy, she has given speeches and workshops at national and international events; and has appeared on numerous radio and television programs, including MSNBC and NPR. She is also the author of *Neptune's Gift: Discovering Your Inner Ocean* (available on Amazon).

The former U.S. Marine photojournalist and forest firefighter holds an interdisciplinary master's degree in Humanities with an emphasis on Human Violence, and a graduate certificate in Women's Studies from Old Dominion University.

Named one of the "Happy 100" people on the planet, CJ's story is featured in two bestselling books, including *Happy for No Reason* and *Be Invincible*.

If you enjoyed this book, please post a review on Amazon to encourage others to read it and protect themselves too.

Sign up for CJ Scarlet's video blog at www.cjscarlet.com that shows you many of the techniques she suggests in *The Badass Girl's Guide*.

To reach CJ Scarlet for media inquiries and speaking opportunities, or to talk with her about her books, contact her at cj@cjscarlet.com.

Acknowledgements

I OWE A great deal of thanks to the many people who read the manuscript and offered gentle suggestions for improvement. To Patrick McCullough, who helped me create the title for this book, you rock!

I owe a special debt of gratitude to Tracy Crow, my muse and bff, for inspiring me to be a better person; my sister Susan for her wise words and courageous example, and to Mary Cantando my mentor and friend, for sharing her wisdom and teaching me how to be a total badass!

Finally, I offer gratitude for my family, especially my grandchildren. I hope you read every word of this book and never need to apply it.

Resources

BELOW IS A list of great resources that can help you learn more about sexual assault, and what to do if you are victimized, as well as support services that are available to you. This is not a comprehensive list; there are literally thousands of support networks that operate at the local, campus, state, and national levels. A simple Internet search will help you find services in your local area.

The two best resources to check out first are the National Sexual Violence Resource Center (www.nsvrc.org) and RAINN, the Rape, Abuse and Incest National Network (www.rainn.org). Both contain links to other organizations that can support you. RAINN also has a toll-free number [800-656-HOPE (4673)] and access to an online chat hotline at https://hotline.rainn.org/online/.

Other Resources

American Association of University Women (www.aauw.org)

Bureau of Justice Statistics (www.bjs.gov)

Crisis resources by state (www.rainn.org)

Definitions of rape and rape terms (www.rainn.org/articles/legal-role-consent)

End Rape on Campus (www.endrapeoncampus.org)

Faculty Against Rape (www.facultyagainstrape.net)

Greeks Against Sexual Assault (www.gasanow.celect.org/coalition)

It Gets Better Project (www.itgetsbetter.org)

Know Your IX (www.knowyourix.org)

Lambda (www.lambdalegal.org)

National Alliance to End Sexual Violence (www.endsexualviolence.
org)

National LGBTQ Taskforce – Be You (www.thetaskforce.org/)

National Organization of Women (www.now.org)

National Student Coalition Against Rape (www.studentcoalition-
againstrape.org)

National Women's Law Center (www.nwlc.org)

NoMore.org (www.nomore.org)

Not Alone (www.notalone.gov)

Not on Our Grounds (UVA) (http://notonourgrounds.virginia.edu/)

One in Four (www.oneinfourusa.org)

One Less (www.atuva.student.virginia.edu/organization/oneless)

Planned Parenthood (www.plannedparenthood.org)

Rainbow Youth Hotline [877/LGBT-YTH (542-8984)]

Raliance Program - National Sexual Violence Resource Center (www.
nsvrc.org)

Students Active for Ending Rape (www.safercampus.org)

Summary of DOJ Statute of Limitations by State (www.studentcoali-
tionagainstrape.org/rape-laws-by-state.html)

Surv Justice - Attorney Advocacy Firm (www.survjustice.org)

Survivor Project (www.survivorproject.org)

Title IX - Office of Civil Rights, Department of Education (www2.
ed.gov/about/offices/list/ocr/docs/tix_dis.html)

U.S. Department of Justice (www.usdoj.gov)

Ultra Violet (www.weareultraviolet.org)

Victim Rights Law Center (www.victimrights.org)

End Notes

i.   www.jasonkatz.com

ii.   Resistance to Violent Crime: What Does the Research Show? Posted on June 23, 2014, by Greg Ellifritz.

iii.   Chuck O'Neill and Kate O'Neill, "Psychological Self-Defense: How to Protect Yourself from Predators, Criminals and Sociopaths Before They Attack."

iv.   iii Acta Obstetricia et Gynecologica Scandinavica, Tonic immobility during sexual assault – a common reaction predicting post-traumatic stress disorder and severe depression, June 22, 2017.

v.   Source unknown.

vi.   iv From a 20-year study conducted from 1973 to 1992 by the National Crime Victimization Survey.

vii.   Ibid.

viii.   U.S. Department of Justice, Bureau of Justice Statistics. "Weapon Use and Violent Crime", September 2003.

ix.   The Efficacy of Women's Resistance Strategies in Rape Situations, Sarah E. Ullman, Raymond A. Knight, Brandeis University.

x.   U.S. Department of Justice, National Crime Victimization Study, 2009-2013.

xi.   U.S. Department of Justice, Bureau of Statistics, Sex Offenses and Offenders Study (1997).

xii.   Date and Acquaintance Rape, Sheryl Huff, ed., Minnesota Coalition for Sexual Assault.

xiii.   xi David Lisak and Paul M. Miller, Repeat Rape and Multiple Offending Among Undetected Rapists.

xiv.   http://www.bjs.gov/index.cfm?ty=tp&tid=317.

xv.   U.S. Department of Justice, Bureau of Justice Statistics. "Weapon Use and Violent Crime," September 2003.

xvi.   Ibid.

xvii.   http://jmm.sagepub.com/content/12/3/275.abstract.

xviii.   Greg Ellifritz, "From Resistance to Violent Crime: What Does the Research Show?"

xix.   National Violence Against Women Survey, 2000. https://www.ncjrs.gov/pdffiles1/nij/183781.pdf.

xx.   Tjaden, P., & Thoennes, N. (2000). Full report of the prevalence, incidence, and consequences of violence against women: Findings from the National Violence Against Women Survey (NCJ 183781). Retrieved from the U.S. Department of Justice, Office of Justice Programs, National Institute of Justice: https://www.ncjrs.gov/pdffiles1/nij/183781.pdf.

xxi.   Muehlenhard et al. (1998); Testa and Derman (1999).

xxii.   Lalumiere et al. (2005); Soothill et al. (2002).

xxiii.   Savino and Turvey (2005); Lalumiere et al. (2005).

xxiv.   Rozee and Koss (2001); Abbey et al. (2007).

xxv.   Davies, Wittebrood and Jackson (1998); Soothill et al. (2002); Goldstein and Susmilch (1982).

xxvi.   MacLellan and Cain (2008).

xxvii.   Rape, Incest & Abuse National Network, www.rainn.org

xxviii. Ibid.

xxix.   Ibid.

xxx.   Ibid.

xxxi.   Federal Bureau of Investigation (2009).

xxxii.   Myhill and Allen (2002).

xxxiii. Davies and Dale (1995).

xxxiv. Ibid.

xxxv. Ibid.

xxxvi. U.S. Department of Justice, National Crime Victimization Study: 2009-2013.

xxxvii. Centers for Disease Control, http://www.cdc.gov/mmwr/preview/mmwrhtml/ss6308a1.htm.

xxxviii. Ibid.

xxxix. Ibid.

xl. Ibid.

xli. Rape and Sexual Assault: A Renewed Call to Action, The White House Council on Women and Girls January 2014. xli Sam Harris, November 5, 2011, The Truth about Violence: 3 Principles of Self-Defense.

xlii. Rhode Island Rape Crisis Center Surveys, 1988 and 1998.

xliii. Abbey et al, 1998.

xliv. Ibid.

xlv. Ibid.

xlvi. http://www.niaaa.nih.gov/alcohol-health/special-populations-co-occurring-disorders/college-drinking.

xlvii. Abbey et al, 1996.

xlviii. http://pubs.niaaa.nih.gov/publications/CollegeFactSheet/CollegeFactSheet.pdf.

xlix. http://www.collegedrinkingprevention.gov/media/journal/118-abbey.pdf.

l. An Examination of Sexual Violence Against College Women.

li.   David Cantor, Bonnie Fisher, Susan Chibnall, Reanna Townsend, et al, Association of American Universities, Report on the AAU Campus Climate Survey on Sexual Assault and Sexual Misconduct, Sept. 21, 2015.

lii.   Ibid.

liii.   www.rainn.org.

liv.   Ibid.

lv.   Ibid.

lvi.   www.oneinfourusa.org.

lvii.   U.S. Department of Justice, 2002.

lviii.   Rape and Sexual Assault: A Renewed Call to Action, The White House Council on Women and Girls January 2014.

lix.   www.ilo.org.

lx.   www.polarisproject.org.

lxi.   Ibid.

lxii.   http://cybersafewomen.org/how_cyber_criminals_and_predators_select_their_prey.

lxiii.   Ibid.

lxiv.   Ibid.

lxv.   Wolak, Janis, David Finkelhor, and Kimberly J. Mitchell, "Internet-Initiated Sex Crimes Against Minors: Implications for Prevention Based on Findings from a National Study," Journal of Adolescent Health, 2004, Vol. 35 (No. 5), pp. 11–20. (http://www.unh.edu/ccrc/pdf/CV71.pdf) November 11, 2010.

lxvi.   www.polarisproject.org

lxvii.   www.rainn.org.

lxviii. http://www.un.org/en/women/endviolence/pdf/VAW.pdf.

lxix.   www.rainn.org.

lxx.   David Lisak and Paul M. Miller, Repeat Rape and Multiple Offending Among Undetected Rapists.

lxxi.   Foundation for Economic Education. http://fee.org/freeman/just-dial-911-the-myth-of-police-protection/.

lxxii. www.knowyourix.org.

lxxiii. http://www2.ed.gov/about/offices/list/ocr/complaintintro.html

lxxiv. http://www.endthebacklog.org/information-survivors-dna-and-rape-kit-evidence/what-rape-kit-and-rape-kit-exam#sthash.3w0xYyRh.dpuf.

lxxv.   Copyright © Marie De Santis, Women's Justice Center. www.justicewomen.com.

lxxvi. Ibid.

lxxvii. Ibid.

lxxviii. Ibid.

lxxix. https://rainn.org/get-information/legal-information/testifying-criminal-trial.

lxxx.   http://www.victimsofcrime.org/docs/Public%20Folders/Civil%20Justice%20-%20FINAL%20(non-book).pdf?sfvrsn=0.

lxxxi. Ira H. Leesfield. http://www.leesfield.com/damages-in-rape-and-sexual-abuse-cases.html.

lxxxii. http://www.mayoclinic.org/diseases-conditions/post-traumatic-stress-disorder/basics/symptoms/con-20022540.

lxxxiii. National Crime Victim Survey, 2015.

lxxxiv. http://www.mayoclinic.org/diseases-conditions/post-traumatic-stress-disorder/basics/risk-factors/con-20022540.

lxxxv. National Crime Victim Survey, 2013.

Made in the USA
Columbia, SC
30 August 2018